BROOKLYN TWEED'S

KNIT &
CROCHET
BLANKETS

For my father, Jeff Flood,
whose beautiful soul
left our world during the
creation of this book.

Dad – I love you.
I miss you. Thank you.

BROOKLYN TWEED'S

KNIT & CROCHET BLANKETS

projects to stitch for home and away

JARED FLOOD

abrams, new york

CONTENTS

03 COLORPLAY

introduction

Most of my earliest memories of childhood contain a backdrop of handmade textiles: drawerfuls of hand-stitched quilts in tonal batiks, warm knitted and crocheted afghans in shades of natural wool unfurled over the couch, handsewn shirts and pants (usually in coordinating fabrics) that my older brothers and I would wear proudly into the world of eighties fashion. My mother was and is a boundless well of textile passion and creativity, and her choice to share these gifts with our family added layers of meaning to my childhood that I still cherish today. As a highly sensitive and tactile young person, I found special power in snuggling under one of my mom's handmade creations. Memories of their texture and even their scent are still vivid. On some level, I understood that these cozy and beautiful fabrics came from many loving hours of stitching and care, well before I could appreciate such things from a technical perspective.

While my mother's expansive quilting, knitting, and crocheting pursuits nurtured my deep love of color, pattern, and texture, more than anything else I remember the feelings they inspired. The power that handmade objects had to make me feel cared for and safe was deeply comforting, and this has been something I've striven to achieve in my own home as an adult.

I've worked as a yarn and textile designer for the better part of two decades and find that these sense memories from childhood still drive much of my creative work today. Knitting and crocheting—as with most forms of handwork—are slow, mindful processes that have the power to infuse everyday objects with deep meaning. I created this book in hopes of giving knitters and crocheters more opportunities to infuse meaning into their lives and homes through craft.

I reflect often on how much the handmade home environment that I grew up in has shaped not only my creative pursuits and my career, but also the things I value about my living space. For me, home is a refuge: a safe place to fully be yourself, a place to share food and conversation with the people who mean the most to you, a nest for recharging and healing, and best of all a place where we grow and learn. Knitting and crochet are wonderful ways to cultivate this kind of presence at home and serve as a form of meditation and centering for many crafters, including myself.

The twenty-five designs in this book are the work of sixteen designers who have joined me in collaboration—along with four creations of my own. While the patterns here will provide enjoyable knitting or crocheting as written, the photographs and creative concepts in the book are meant to inspire your own unique exploration and creativity. Blankets are blank canvases for your ideas, and I hope this collection gives you a taste of what you can do when exploring this genre. So here's to many cozy evenings on, under, or in the midst of making your next family heirloom.

7

how to use this book

I designed this book like a recipe box: The patterns can be drawn from for years to come and invite variation and personalization. Handmade blankets are meaningful heirlooms to be shared and enjoyed by multiple generations, and are also a commitment of time, materials, and money. Providing as much pattern flexibility as possible was important to me, in hopes that it would allow readers to create a version of each blanket that most suits their needs, preferences, and budget.

aesthetic themes

The book is divided into three aesthetic themes: Traditions, Minimalism, and Colorplay. Your home's interior may align closely with one theme more than the others, or you may be inspired to pick and choose favorites from across the chapters. I encourage you to explore and make the designs that feel like the best fit for you and your spaces.

skill level

Patterns with a range of skill levels have been included throughout the book so that, no matter your level of experience, you can make beautiful projects for the home. Each pattern features a skill level indicator (1–5) that will help you determine the right project for your abilities. Skill level 1 projects are perfect for beginners, while skill level 5 is aimed at advanced knitters.

The majority of patterns in the book fall in the range of beginner to intermediate, with a few advanced projects like traditional lace (page 33) or heavily cabled fabrics (page 15) spicing up the mix.

sizing

baby blankets	
cradle	15 x 30" (38 x 76 cm)
stroller	30 x 36" (76 x 91 cm)
swaddler	48 x 48" (122 x 122 cm)

throws	
lap blanket	36 x 48" (91 x 122 cm)
small throw	48 x 60" (122 x 152 cm)
large throw	60 x 72" (152 x 183 cm)

bed coverings		mattress dimension
crib	42 x 52" (107 x 132 cm)	28 x 52" (71 x 132 cm)
twin bed	60 x 90" (152 x 229 cm)	38 x 75" (97 x 191 cm)
full bed	84 x 90" (213 x 229 cm)	53 x 75" (135 x 191 cm)
queen bed	90 x 96" (229 x 244 cm)	60 x 80" (152 x 203 cm)
king bed	118 x 96" (300 x 244 cm)	76 x 80" (193 x 203 cm)

Most of the patterns include multiple sizing options and provide yardage requirements for each size presented. Other patterns offer suggestions for ways to change the size or appearance (adding multiple colors, for example) of a given blanket and are meant to function as a creative springboard for your imagination.

All the blankets adhere as closely as possible to the standard sizing chart shown here. This table is a helpful resource when planning what size blanket will be needed for your intended application (twin or queen bed? stroller or crib size?). The chart will also be helpful in supplying target measurements if you go "off pattern" and modify one of the designs to your own liking.

Several of the blankets are rectangles worked end-to-end with little or no shaping, so changing their width or length is as easy as casting on extra stitches for additional repeats or working a longer or shorter length. Patterns for nontraditionally shaped blankets (center-out circular lace, quilt-block-style construction, etc.) offer additional suggestions on sizing and design modifications where applicable.

Putting our personal stamp on the things we create with our hands is one of the great joys of being a maker. I encourage you to explore and interpret the patterns in the book freely to create beautiful, one-of-a-kind heirlooms that you'll use lovingly for years and pass along to future generations.

digital appendix for written instructions
If you prefer working from written line-by-line instructions rather than charts, those can be found online in the Digital Appendix, for all the projects in this book that include charts: https://brooklyntweed.com/pages/knit-and-crochet-blankets-appendix

TRADITIO

NS

01

These designs call upon knitting's rich heritage, using traditional techniques and textures that infuse a sense of timelessness into the heart of the home.

Cables, lace, and other textured stitches celebrate history and tradition. Designs in this chapter are perfect for cozy, woolen-spun tweed and heathered yarns that mimic the colors and textures found in nature.

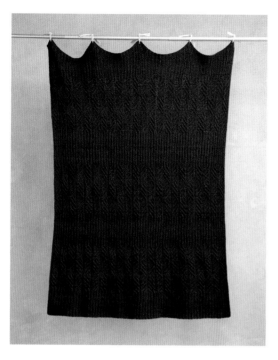

branching 15

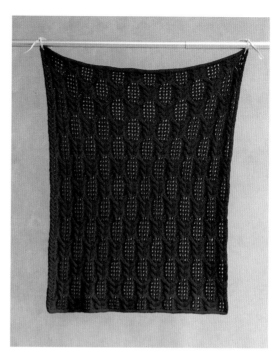

coutume 21

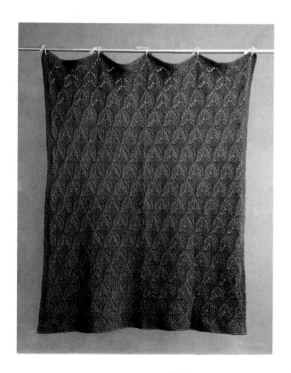

umaro 27

permafrost 33

goodnight star 43

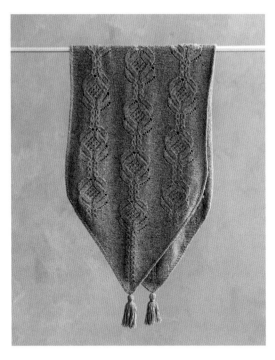

winterly 49

rattan 57

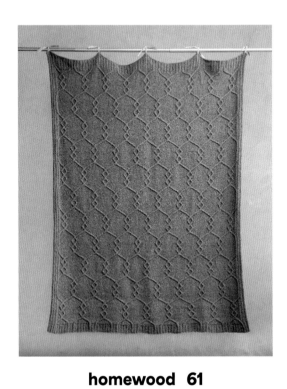

homewood 61

branching

designed by Amy van de Laar

This sumptuous, cabled blanket feels both traditional and modern with alternating banded blocks of lush cables and clean vertical ribbing. Worked in a smooth, springy five-ply merino yarn, the motifs are carved in relief-like detail. The lush unfolding cables were inspired by the natural symmetry of leaves and branching trees and bring echoes of the great outdoors into the heart of the home. The cable motifs are satisfying and absorbing to knit, while sections of ribbing provide breathing space (and welcoming periods of mindless stitching in between!).

yardage table

blanket size	yardage required	
	yards	meters
lap blanket	1538	1406
small throw	2726	2493
large throw	3713	3395

PATTERN SPECS

yarn
- Worsted-weight wool yarn
- Small Throw size shown in Brooklyn Tweed Imbue (104 yards/50 g) in color "Cloak"

gauge
- 23 stitches & 23 rows = 4" [10 cm] in blocked Rib Pattern
- 23 stitches & 25½ rows = 5" [12.5 cm] in blocked Branching Pattern

needles
One 40" [100 cm] or longer circular needle in size needed to obtain gauge
- Suggested size: US 7/4.5 mm

notions and tools
- Cable needle in smaller size than working needle
- Locking stitch markers
- Blunt tapestry needle
- T-pins and blocking wires (optional)

stitch pattern

rib pattern
Worked over a multiple of 4 of stitches + 2; 2-row repeat

row 1 (RS): {S2SS}, *purl 2, knit 2; repeat from * to end.

row 2 (WS): {S2SS}, *knit 2, purl 2; repeat from * to last 4 stitches, knit 4.

Repeat Rows 1 and 2 for pattern.

skill level
●●●○○
Intermediate

finished sizes
lap blanket
- W: 34½" × L: 47¼"
- W: 87.5 cm × L: 120 cm

small throw
- W: 47" × L: 61¾"
- W: 119.5 cm × L: 157 cm

large throw
- W: 55¼" × L: 71"
- W: 140.5 cm × L: 180.5 cm

sizing notes
- The blanket width can be adjusted by adding or subtracting stitches in increments of 24.
- Adjusting the blanket's size will affect the total yardage requirements for the project.

special techniques
- Two-Stitch Slipped Selvedge {S2SS}: page 188
- Reading Charts: page 186
- Blocking: page 182

PATTERN INSTRUCTIONS

Cast on 198 (270, 318) stitches using your preferred method. For this pattern, we recommend the Long-Tail Cast-On.

tip: If casting on using the Long-Tail method, you can avoid running out of yarn by beginning with two skeins of yarn and tying their ends together to create the initial slipknot. If you have a center-pull yarn ball, you can use both ends of the same ball instead. Break the second strand of yarn after all stitches have been cast on.

setup row (WS): Knit 2, *knit 2, purl 2; repeat from * to last 4 stitches, knit 4.

Place a locking stitch marker in one of the stitches of the Setup Row.

rib section

Work Rows 1 and 2 of Rib Pattern (see Stitch Pattern) 24 (20, 27) times, for a total of 48 (40, 54) rows after the locking stitch marker.

cable section

Work Rows 1–72 of Branching Pattern (from chart on page 19 or written instructions in Digital Appendix) one time.

Place a locking stitch marker in one of the stitches of the last row worked.

Repeat from Rib Section 1 (2, 2) more time(s) for a total of 2 (3, 3) Rib Sections and 2 (3, 3) Cable Sections worked.

rib section

Work Rows 1 and 2 of Rib Pattern 22 (18, 25) times for a total of 44 (36, 50) rows after the locking stitch marker.

Bind off all stitches in pattern from the RS, slipping the first 2 stitches with yarn held in front.

finishing

Weave in ends invisibly on the WS. For a polished finish, steam- or wet-block (see Special Techniques on page 182) the blanket to the finished dimensions for your chosen size to set the fabric.

SYMBOL LEGEND

Knit
Knit stitch on RS; purl stitch on WS

Purl
Purl stitch on RS; knit stitch on WS

Slip wyif
Slip 1 stitch purlwise with yarn in front

2/2 LC (Left Cross)
Slip 2 stitches to CN and hold in front,
knit 2 stitches from L needle,
knit 2 stitches from CN

2/2 RC (Right Cross)
Slip 2 stitches to CN and hold in back,
knit 2 stitches from L needle,
knit 2 stitches from CN

2/2 LCp (Left Cross over purl)
Slip 2 stitches to CN and hold in front,
purl 2 stitches from L needle,
knit 2 stitches from CN

2/2 RCp (Right Cross over purl)
Slip 2 stitches to CN and hold in back,
knit 2 stitches from L needle,
purl 2 stitches from CN

Repeat
Stitches within brackets
create the pattern repeat

BRANCHING CHART

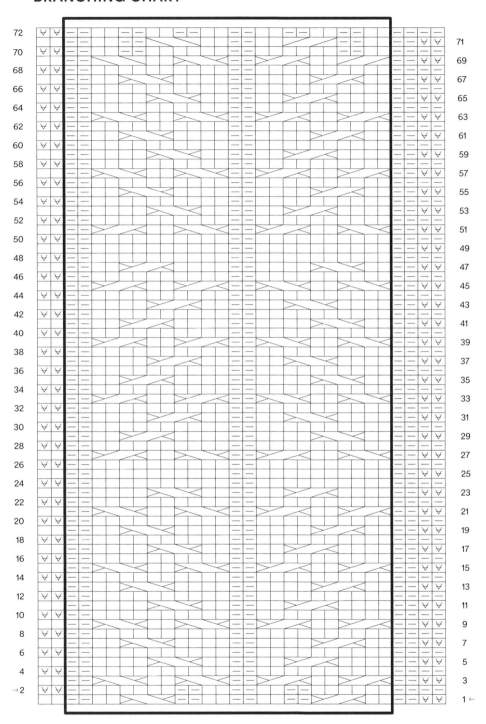

24-stitch repeat

coutume

designed by Emma Ducher

Coutume–French for tradition, habit, or custom–is a timeless, delicately textured baby blanket that mixes Aran cabling traditions with eyelet lace motifs for a fabric that is both textural and light. The tidy I-cord cast-on forms a polished foundation for the blanket, which continues directly into the blanket's edging and through to an I-cord bind-off finish. This cleanly trimmed piece is a joy to work for detail lovers and results in a handsome fabric that will be worthy of any newborn's sacred presence in our world.

yardage table

blanket size	yardage required	
	yards	meters
cradle	499	456
stroller	1208	1105
lap blanket	1959	1791

skill level

●●●○○
Intermediate

finished sizes

cradle blanket
• W: 15½" × L: 30"
• W: 39.5 cm × L: 76 cm

stroller blanket
• W: 31¼" × L: 36"
• W: 79.5 cm × L: 91.5 cm

lap blanket
• W: 38" × L: 48"
• W: 96.5 cm × L: 122 cm

special techniques

• Provisional Crochet Cast-On: page 186
• Reading Charts: page 186
• Grafting: page 183
• Blocking: page 182

PATTERN SPECS

yarn

• DK-weight wool yarn
• Cradle Blanket size shown in Brooklyn Tweed Re•Ply Rambouillet (130 yards/ 45 g) in color "Root"
• Stroller Blanket size shown in Brooklyn Tweed Arbor (145 yards/50 g) in color "Alizarin"

gauge

23 stitches & 28 rows = 4" [10 cm] in blocked Coutume Pattern

needles

One 32" [80 cm] or longer circular needle in size needed to obtain gauge
• Suggested size: US 6/4 mm

notions and tools

• Size US G-6/4 mm crochet hook and smooth waste yarn (for Provisional Crochet Cast-On)
• Cable needle
• Blunt tapestry needle
• T-pins and blocking wires (optional)

PATTERN INSTRUCTIONS

i-cord cast-on

With waste yarn, cast on 5 stitches using the Provisional Crochet Cast-On (see Special Techniques on page 186). Switch to working yarn.

row 1 (RS): *Knit 5; slip the 5 stitches back to the L needle, pulling the working yarn behind the stitches.

Repeat from *, forming an I-cord, for a total of 79 (170, 209) rows.

next row (RS): Slip the 5 stitches back to the L needle, pulling the working yarn behind the stitches, knit 5, and pick up and knit 79 (170, 209) stitches along the I-cord until you reach the provisional cast-on. Remove waste yarn and knit the 5 provisional stitches. [89 (180, 219) stitches now on needle]

note: Next row is a WS row.

main fabric

Begin Coutume Pattern (from charts on pages 24 and 25 or written instructions in Digital Appendix) for your size; work until piece measures 29½ (35½, 47½)" [75 (90, 120.5 cm], ending with a RS row.

i-cord bind-off

next row: *Knit 4, k2tog-tbl; slip 5 stitches back to the L needle, pulling the working yarn behind the stitches. Repeat from * until 5 stitches remain on both needles.

Break yarn, leaving an 8" [20.5 cm] tail.

Thread the yarn tail on the tapestry needle.

Place the 2 needles facing each other with RS together and working yarn to the right and join stitches using Grafting (see Special Techniques on page 183).

finishing

Weave in ends invisibly on the WS. For a polished finish, steam- or wet-block (see Special Techniques on page 182) the blanket to the finished dimensions for your chosen size to set the fabric.

CHART: Cradle & Lap Blanket

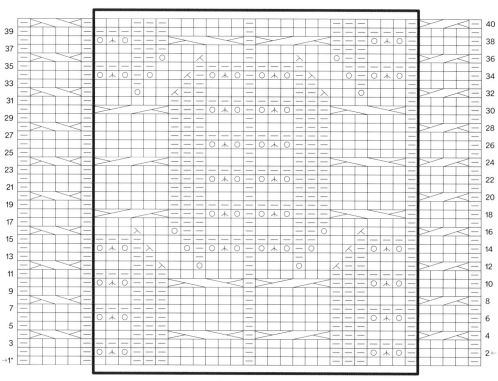

26-stitch repeat

*Note that Row 1 is a WS row.

SYMBOL LEGEND

☐ **Knit**
Knit stitch on RS; purl stitch on WS

— **Purl**
Purl stitch on RS; knit stitch on WS

○ **YO**
With yarn in front, bring yarn over top of R needle from front to back, creating a yarn over (1 stitch increased)

✕ **K2tog**
Knit two stitches from L needle together, creating a right-leaning decrease

✕ **SSK**
Slip 1 stitch knitwise from L to R needle, replace stitch on L needle in new orientation then knit 2 stitches together through the back loops, creating a left-leaning decrease

⅄ **RDD (Raised Double Decrease)**
Slip 2 stitches from L to R needle at the same time as if to knit 2 together, knit 1 from L needle, pass the slipped stitches over stitch just worked (2 stitches decreased; centered)

✕ **2/2 LC (Left Cross)**
Slip 2 stitches to CN and hold in front, knit 2 stitches from L needle, knit 2 stitches from CN

24

CHART: Stroller Blanket

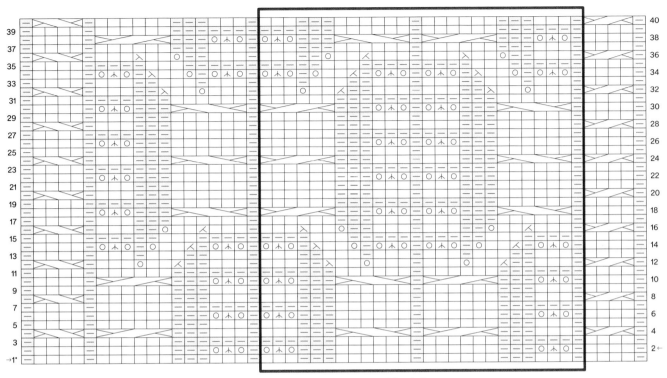

*Note that Row 1 is a WS row.

26-stitch repeat

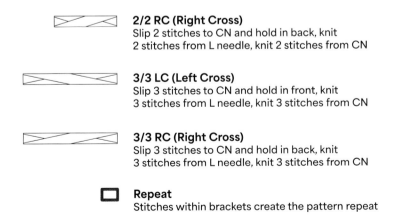

2/2 RC (Right Cross)
Slip 2 stitches to CN and hold in back, knit
2 stitches from L needle, knit 2 stitches from CN

3/3 LC (Left Cross)
Slip 3 stitches to CN and hold in front, knit
3 stitches from L needle, knit 3 stitches from CN

3/3 RC (Right Cross)
Slip 3 stitches to CN and hold in back, knit
3 stitches from L needle, knit 3 stitches from CN

Repeat
Stitches within brackets create the pattern repeat

25

umaro

designed by Jared Flood

Umaro combines a little bit of everything—cables, lace, and knit-purl patterns—to create rhythmic textures that are every bit as soothing to knit as they are to curl up under. Yarn overs and directional decreases flow into staggered cables that form an allover diamond pattern, while delicate seed stitch provides a soft, pebbly backdrop for the geometric motif. Umaro has been a fan favorite for more than a decade at Brooklyn Tweed, and I've included the pattern here with instructions to knit a range of finished sizes using DK, worsted, or bulky yarn. Use the pattern as a recipe to make as many variations as you'd like!

yardage table

blanket size	DK version		worsted version		chunky version	
	yards	meters	yards	meters	yards	meters
stroller	942	861	789	721	793	725
small throw	2150	1966	1870	1710	1935	1769
large throw	3984	3643	3584	3277	3878	3546

PATTERN SPECS

yarn
- DK-, worsted-, or chunky-weight wool yarn
- DK version Stroller Blanket size shown in Brooklyn Tweed Re•Ply Rambouillet (130 yards/45 g) in color "Olive Oil"
- Chunky version Large Throw size shown in Brooklyn Tweed Quarry (200 yards/100 g) held double in color "Slate"

gauge
- DK version: 16 stitches & 28 rows = 4" [10 cm] in blocked Seed Stitch
- One 12-stitch repeat of Umaro Pattern measures 2½" [6 cm] wide after blocking
- Worsted version: 16 stitches & 32 rows = 4" [10 cm] in blocked Seed Stitch
- One 12-stitch repeat of Umaro Pattern measures 3" [7.5 cm] wide after blocking
- Chunky version: 8 stitches & 16 rows = 4" [10 cm] with yarn held double in blocked Seed Stitch
- One 12-stitch repeat of Umaro Pattern with yarn held double measures 5" [12 cm] wide after blocking

notions and tools
- Two cable needles
- Blunt tapestry needle
- T-pins and blocking wires (optional)

skill level
●●○○○
Adventurous Beginner

finished sizes
Measurements vary slightly depending on yarn weight used. See Sizing Matrix for exact dimensions.

stroller blanket
- W: 29" × L: 36"
- W: 73.5 cm × L: 91.5 cm

small throw
- W: 44" × L: 56"
- W: 112 cm × L: 142 cm

large throw
- W: 63" × L: 75"
- W: 160 cm × L: 190.5 cm

special techniques
- Reading Charts: page 186
- Blocking: page 182

needles
One 40" [100 cm] or longer circular needle in size needed to obtain gauge
- Suggested size for DK version: US 7/4.5 mm
- Suggested size for Worsted version: US 9/5.5 mm
- Suggested size for Chunky version: US 13/9 mm

sizing matrix

	finished dimensions	A cast on	B pattern repeats over 28 rows	C motif repeats over 12 stitches
DK version	29½" (75 cm) wide; 37" (94 cm) long	139 stitches	9	10
	44½" (113 cm) wide; 56" (142 cm) long	211 stitches	14	16
	62" (157 cm) wide; 74½" (189 cm) long	295 stitches	19	23
worsted version	29" (74 cm) wide; 35½" (90 cm) long	115 stitches	8	8
	44" (112 cm) wide; 55½" (141 cm) long	175 stitches	13	13
	62" (157 cm) wide; 75½" (192 cm) long	247 stitches	18	19
chunky version	29" (74 cm) wide; 34½" (88 cm) long	67 stitches	4	4
	44" (112 cm) wide; 55½" (141 cm) long	103 stitches	7	7
	64" (163 cm) wide; 76½" (194 cm) long	151 stitches	10	11

pattern notes

- This pattern is written for three weights of yarn, and for three sizes for each yarn. Refer to the Sizing Matrix for exact finished dimensions of the version you are working.
- The pattern is supplied with blank spaces to represent numbers found in the Sizing Matrix. Before knitting the pattern, transfer the numbers for the version you are working from the Sizing Matrix into the blank spaces provided in the pattern.
- The chunky-version sample has been knit with two strands of chunky yarn held together throughout but may also be worked with a single strand of bulky-weight yarn to achieve the same gauge.

chart notes

- The 12-stitch motif repeats C_____ times on every row.
- Some symbols have instructions for both RS and WS of work. Symbols that have only one instruction only ever fall on the RS.

PATTERN INSTRUCTIONS

Cast on **A**_____ stitches using your preferred method. For this pattern, we recommend the Long-Tail Cast-On, but any cast-on will work.

tip: If casting on using the Long-Tail method, you can avoid running out of yarn by beginning with two skeins of yarn and tying their ends together to create the initial slipknot. If you have a center-pull yarn ball, you can use both ends of the same ball instead. Break the second strand of yarn after all stitches have been cast on.

setup row (WS): *Knit 1, purl 1; repeat from * to last stitch, knit 1.

row 1 (RS): *Knit 1, purl 1; repeat from * to last stitch, knit 1.

Work 4 rows even in established Seed Stitch pattern, ending with a RS row.

next row (WS): Knit 1, purl 1, knit 1, purl 6, knit 1, purl 8, *purl 3, knit 1, purl 8; repeat from * to last 13 stitches, purl 3, knit 1, purl 6, knit 1, purl 1, knit 1.

Work Rows 1–28 of Umaro Pattern (from chart on page 31 or written instructions in Digital Appendix) **B**_____ times total. Note that the 12-stitch bracketed repeat in the chart is worked **C**_____ times on every row.

After completing the final repeat of Umaro Pattern, work Rows 1–14 one more time.

next row (RS): Knit 1, purl 1, knit 1, purl 1, *knit 5, purl 1; repeat from * to last 3 stitches, knit 1, purl 1, knit 1.

next row (WS): *Knit 1, purl 1; repeat from * to last stitch, knit 1. Work 5 rows even in established Seed Stitch pattern, ending with a RS row.

Bind off all stitches in pattern.

finishing

Weave in ends invisibly on the WS. For a polished finish, steam- or wet-block the blanket to the finished dimensions for your chosen yarn weight and size to set the fabric (see Special Techniques on page 182).

UMARO CHART

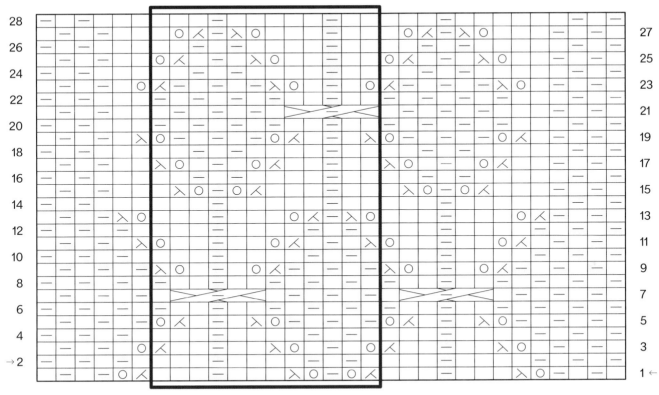

12 stitch repeat

SYMBOL LEGEND

Knit
Knit stitch on RS; purl stitch on WS

Purl
Purl stitch on RS; knit stitch on WS

YO
With yarn in front, bring yarn over top of R needle from front to back, creating a yarn over (1 stitch increased)

K2tog
On RS knit 2 stitches together; on WS purl 2 stitches together (1 stitch decreased; leans right)

SSK (modified)
On RS slip 1 stitch knitwise from L to R needle, replace stitch on L needle in new orientation then knit two stitches together through the back loops; on WS slip 2 stitches knitwise one at a time from L to R needle, return these stitches to L needle in their new orientation and purl them together through their back loops (1 stitch decreased; leans left)

2/1/2 RCp
Slip 2 stitches to CN and hold in back, slip next stitch to second CN and hold in back, knit 2 from L needle (keeping second CN in back), purl 1 from second CN, knit 2 from first CN

Repeat
Stitches within brackets create the pattern repeat

permafrost

designed by Jared Flood

When I was first starting my career in knitwear design, I loved taking traditional lace shawl patterns from the early twentieth century and working them in heavier, wooly yarns to create blankets that amped up the sculptural qualities of the fabric. Permafrost was designed with this idea in mind, employing sinewy plant-like stitch patterns that unfurl as you knit. Worked from the center out, the circular blanket is worked in the round and—with the exception of sections 5 and 6—has a plain round of knitting between each lace round, creating a nice balance between mindless and mindful knitting. While shown as a small throw in worsted-weight yarn, the finished size and weight of the blanket can be easily changed by exploring the use of different yarn weights; try anything from laceweight to chunky.

skill level
●●●●○
Adventurous Intermediate

finished size
<u>small throw</u>
• Diameter: 58"
• Diameter: 147 cm

sizing note
Dimensions can be adjusted by working in a thinner or thicker yarn and working the pattern as written.

special techniques
• Circular Cast-On: page 182
• Reading Charts: page 186
• Provisional Crochet Cast-On: page 186
• Grafting: page 183
• Blocking: page 182

yardage table

blanket size	yardage required	
	yards	meters
small throw	1476	1350

The listed yardage requirements will need to be adjusted if changing yarn weight.

PATTERN SPECS

yarn
• Worsted-weight wool yarn
• Shown in Brooklyn Tweed Shelter (140 yards/50 g) in color "Fossil"

gauge
14¾ stitches & 32 rounds = 4" [10 cm] in lace pattern after blocking

needles
One set of double-pointed needles (DPNs), one 32" [80 cm] and one 40" [100 cm] (optional) circular needle in size needed to obtain gauge
• Suggested size: US 8/5 mm

notions and tools
• Size US H-8/5 mm crochet hook and smooth waste yarn (for Provisional Crochet Cast-On)
• Stitch markers
• Blunt tapestry needle
• T-pins for blocking

PATTERN INSTRUCTIONS

With DPNs (or 32" [80 cm] circular, for knitters using the Magic Loop method) cast on 14 stitches using the Circular Cast-On (see Special Techniques on page 182). Distribute the stitches mostly evenly, place a marker, and join work into the round.

note: If working with DPNs, place the first and last stitch of your round on the same needle (with stitch marker in between) so that your marker will not fall off.

section 1

Work Rounds 1–27 of Chart 1 (from chart on page 38 or written instructions in Digital Appendix).

- Chart 1 begins with 2 stitches per repeat and ends, after completion of Round 27, with 20 stitches per repeat.
- Marker placement will change at the end of Round 25. See special instructions for this round below.
- Charts 1–5 are repeated 7 times on every round.

round 25: Knit until 1 stitch remains in round, slip last stitch to R needle, remove marker, return slipped stitch to L needle, replace marker. This indicates the new beginning of round.

Upon completion of Chart 1, you will have 140 stitches on your needles.

section 2

Work Rounds 1–40 of Chart 2 (from chart on page 38 or written instructions in Digital Appendix).

- Chart 2 begins with 20 stitches per repeat before working Round 1 and ends, after completion of Round 40, with 38 stitches per repeat.
- Change to circular needle as soon as the circumference of your work allows you to do so comfortably.

Upon completion of Chart 2, you will have 266 stitches on your needles.

section 3

Work Rounds 1–30 of Chart 3 (from chart on page 40 or written instructions in Digital Appendix).

- Chart 3 begins with 38 stitches per repeat before working Round 1 and ends, after completion of Round 30, with 53 stitches per repeat.
- Bracketed section repeats 2 times per every instance of chart.

Upon completion of Chart 3, you will have 371 stitches on your needles.

section 4

Work Rounds 1–16 of Chart 4 (from chart on page 40 or written instructions in Digital Appendix).

- Chart 4 begins with 53 stitches per repeat before working Round 1 and ends, after completion of Round 16, with 65 stitches per repeat.
- Bracketed section repeats 3 times per every instance of chart.

Upon completion of Chart 4, you will have 455 stitches on your needle.

section 5

Work Rounds of 1–38 of Chart 5 (from chart on page 41 or written instructions in Digital Appendix).

- Chart 5 begins with 65 stitches per repeat before working Round 1 and ends, after completion of Round 38, with 78 stitches per repeat.
- Bracketed section repeats 2 times per every instance of chart.
- Chart 5 involves patterning on both odd- and even-numbered rounds.
- Rounds 33–37 involve special stitches that significantly change your total number of stitches from round to round. Below is a list of the total number of stitches per chart repeat you will have upon completion of each of these rounds:
  + Round 33: 82 stitches per repeat (574 total blanket stitches)

+ Round 34: 92 stitches per repeat (644 total blanket stitches)
+ Round 35: 82 stitches per repeat (574 total blanket stitches)
+ Round 37: 78 stitches per repeat (546 total blanket stitches)

Upon completion of Chart 5, you will have 546 stitches on your needles. You have finished the circular portion of your blanket and will no longer be working in the round. You may now remove your markers, which are no longer needed, and break your working yarn.

knitted-on edging
The edging is worked back and forth, with the final stitch of every RS row being knit together with one live stitch from the blanket perimeter. This technique secures all live stitches without the need for an inelastic bind-off.

With a single DPN and waste yarn, cast on 13 stitches using the Provisional Crochet Cast-On (see Special Techniques on page 186; you may cast on normally, although you will be required to work a small seam in your edging to finish). Switch to working yarn.

With WS of main piece facing, knit across provisionally cast-on stitches. Turn work.

setup row (RS): Knit 1, k2tog, YO, k2tog, YO, k2tog, knit 2, YO, SSK, knit 1. You have one provisional edging stitch remaining–knit this stitch together (as for a k2tog) with the adjacent live stitch from blanket perimeter (this action will hereafter be called "Join").

Work Rows 2–12 of Chart 6 (from chart on page 41 or written instructions in Digital Appendix).

• Chart 6 involves patterning on both RS and WS rows– be sure to review RS and WS instructions within the Legend for all symbols in this chart.
• Every RS/odd-numbered row ends with "Join"–working the final edging stitch together with the next live blanket perimeter stitch. You will consume 6 stitches from the blanket perimeter on every 12-row repeat of Chart 6.
• The first stitch of every WS/even-numbered row is slipped with yarn in front (toward WS).

Repeat Rows 1–12 of Chart 6 until all live stitches from the blanket perimeter have been consumed. You will work Rows 1–12 of Chart 6 a total of 90 times, not including the first instance worked (Rows 2–12).

When you have finished the final repeat of Chart 6, place the 12 live stitches onto a DPN. Carefully unpick the provisional cast-on from the beginning of your edging and slip those 12 stitches (there is always one less stitch than your original cast-on number when returning to a provisional row) onto a second DPN. Break working yarn, leaving a 12" [30.5 cm] tail. With yarn tail, join both sets of 12 live stitches together using Grafting (see Special Techniques on page 183).

finishing
Weave in ends invisibly on the WS. For a polished finish, wet-block the piece to the finished dimensions (see Special Techniques on page 182). Using several T-pins, pin out the blanket to the finished diameter (one pin per edging point is recommended for best results). Let dry completely before unpinning. Remove the pins.

CHART 1

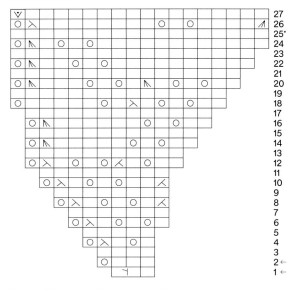

*See written instructions on page 34.

CHART 2

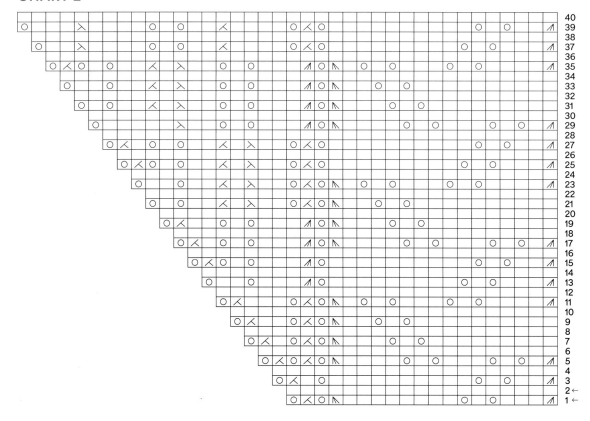

SYMBOL LEGEND

Knit
Knit stitch on RS; purl stitch on WS

Purl
Purl stitch on RS; knit stitch on WS

KFB
Knit into the front and then into the back of the same stitch (1 stitch increased)

YO
With yarn in front, bring yarn over top of R needle from front to back, creating a yarn over (1 stitch increased)

Slip wyif
Slip 1 stitch purlwise with yarn in front

K2tog
On RS knit 2 stitches together; on WS purl 2 stitches together (1 stitch decreased; leans right)

SSK
On RS slip 1 stitch knitwise from L to R needle, replace stitch on L needle in new orientation then knit two stitches together through the back loops; on WS slip 2 stitches knitwise one at a time from L to R needle, return these stitches to L needle in their new orientation and purl them together through their back loops (1 stitch decreased; leans left)

S1K2P
Slip 1 stitch knitwise from L to R needle, knit 2 stitches together from L needle, pass the slipped stitch over the stitch you just worked (2 stitches decreased; leans left)

K3tog
Knit 3 stitches together (2 stitches decreased; leans right)

SSSK
Slip 1 stitch knitwise from L to R needle, replace stitch on L needle in new orientation then knit three stitches together through the back loops (2 stitches decreased; leans left)

RDD (Raised Double Decrease)
Slip 2 stitches from L to R needle at the same time as if to knit 2 together, knit 1 from L needle, pass the slipped stitches over stitch just worked (2 stitches decreased; centered)

K4tog
Knit 4 stitches together (3 stitches decreased; leans right)

SSSSK
Slip 4 stitches separately from L to R needle as if to knit. Replace these stitches on L needle in their new orientation and knit them together through their back loops (3 stitches decreased, leans left)

5-into-5
Knit 5 stitches together ("k5tog") without dropping stitches from L needle, yarn over, k5tog without dropping stitches from needle, yarn over, k5tog again, dropping all 5 stitches from L needle

Open Nupp
[Knit 1, YO, knit 1, YO, knit 1] into the next stitch; for best results, work these stitches loosely (5 stitches created from 1; 4 stitches increased)

Close Nupp R
Knit the 5 nupp stitches (created in the previous round) together (5 stitches decreased to 1)

Close Nupp L
Knit the 5 nupp stitches (created in the previous round) together *through their back loops* (5 stitches decreased to 1)

KPK
Knit 1, purl 1, knit 1 into the same stitch. (2 stitches increased)

M5
[Knit 1, Purl 1 into one stitch] two times, then knit into the front of stitch one more time. (4 stitches increased)

5-to-1
Slip 2 stitches *separately* from L to R needle as if to knit. Knit 2 together from L needle. Pass second stitch on R needle over stitch just made. Slip first stitch on R needle back to L needle. Place R needle tip into second stitch on Left needle and draw it over first stitch of L needle. Slip first stitch on L needle back to right needle. With L needle tip, slip second stitch on R needle over first. (4 stitches decreased)

Double YO
Wrap working yarn around R needle twice, creating two new loops

Edging Join
Knit this edging stitch together (as for k2tog) with adjacent live stitch from blanket circumference

No Stitch
No stitch exists here in your knitting. Ignore this symbol and proceed to next working stitch in row. This symbol is a tool used to keep the chart aligned properly when the stitch count in a row changes.

Repeat
Stitches within brackets are worked more than one time

CHART 3

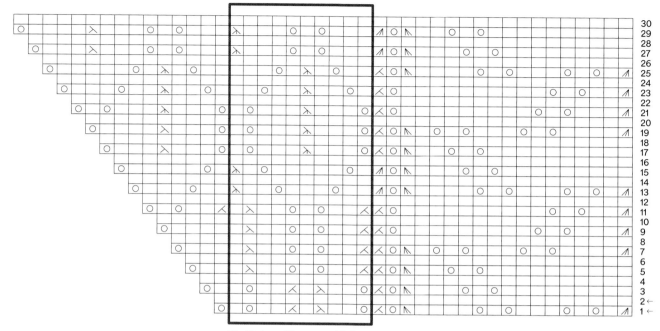

10-stitch motif repeated 2 times

CHART 4

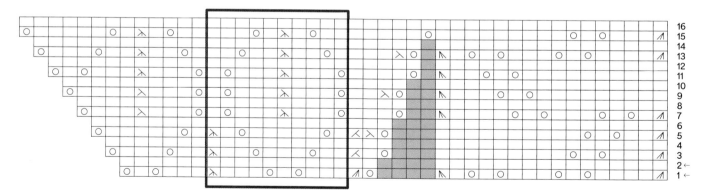

10-stitch motif repeated 3 times

CHART 5

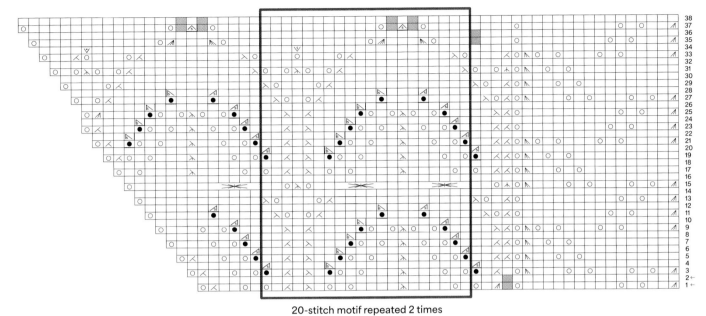

20-stitch motif repeated 2 times

CHART 6

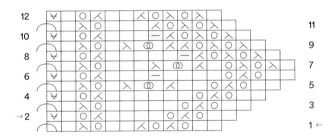

goodnight star

designed by Lis Smith

Crocheting and quilting naturally share a scrappy, no-waste sensibility and a general construction method of easy-to-work smaller segments that are then joined into a larger cohesive whole. This baby blanket reinterprets the familiar granny square into a versatile quilt block, using an unusual construction method to achieve a block with strong diagonals (also known as Half Square Triangles, or HSTs, in quilters' parlance). This particular configuration of HST blocks is called a Sawtooth Star, but many other layouts are possible (see alternative configurations at the end of the pattern). After the internal blocks are seamed, a finishing striped border is crocheted around the outer edge to smooth the seam joins. A single Sawtooth block is the perfect size for a baby blanket (that doubles as a shawl!). If a larger blanket is desired, multiple stars may be made and seamed together before adding the finishing border.

skill level

●●○○○
Adventurous Beginner

finished size

stroller blanket
- 34" square
- 86.25 cm square

Individual Block Size
- Small Block: 6" [15 cm] square
- Large Block: 12" [30.5 cm] square

special techniques
- Blocking: page 182
- Mattress Stitch for Crochet: page 186

yardage table

blanket size	C1		C2		C3		C4	
	yards	meters	yards	meters	yards	meters	yards	meters
stroller	996	911	176	161	203	186	97	89

PATTERN SPECS

yarn
- Fingering-weight wool yarn
- Shown in Brooklyn Tweed Peerie (210 yards/50 g) in colors "Fleet" (C1), "Butte" (C2), "Klimt" (C3), and "Aurora" (C4)

gauge
- Rounds 1–5 = 4" [10 cm] across
- Rounds 1–9 of small Solid Square Block = 6" [15.25 cm], blocked

note: While gauge is not critical, a discrepancy in gauge may affect the yardage used. Check your gauge and adjust hook size if necessary.

hook
Suggested size: US E-4/3.5 mm, or size needed to achieve gauge

notions and tools
- Blunt tapestry needle
- T-pins and blocking wires (optional)

PATTERN INSTRUCTIONS

This blanket is made of thirteen individually crocheted square motifs, which are worked with RS facing throughout. The Sawtooth Star pattern shown in this sample consists of eight crocheted HST blocks, four small solid blocks, and one large solid center block. After blocking, the motifs are then sewn together using the Mattress Stitch for Crochet (see Special Techniques on page 186), as shown in the Assembly Diagram. A simple striped border is worked around the entire blanket once the blocks have been seamed. You may wish to crochet over your ends when possible to cut down on weaving-in during finishing.

block instructions

solid square block

Two sizes of Solid Square Blocks are needed for the blanket layout, a small size and a large size. Work Rounds 1–9 only for the small blocks and work Rounds 1–18 for the large block. Both size blocks will be worked in C1.

Ch 4, Sl st in first ch to form a ring.

round 1 (RS): Ch 3 (counts as 1 dc throughout), 2 dc into ring, [ch 2, 3 dc into ring] 3 times. Join round with sc in 3rd ch of beginning ch-3. (This "joining sc" acts as a ch 1 and leaves the hook in the middle of the resulting space, ready to work the next round.) [4 ch-2 sps]

round 2 (RS): Ch 3, 2 dc in same sp (around the sc), ch 1, [(3 dc, ch 2, 3 dc) in next ch-2 sp, ch 1] 3 times, 3 dc in same sp as beginning ch-3, ch 1. Join round with sc in 3rd ch of the beginning ch-3. [4 ch-2 corner sps; 4 ch-1 sps]

round 3: Ch 3, 2 dc in same sp, ch 1, 3 dc in next ch-sp, ch 1, [(3 dc, ch 2, 3 dc) in next ch-2 sp, ch 1, 3 dc in next ch-1 sp, ch 1] 3 times, 3 dc in same sp as beginning ch-3, ch 1. Join round with sc in 3rd ch of the beginning ch-3. [4 ch-2 corner sps; 8 ch-1 sps]

round 4: Ch 3, 2 dc in same sp, ch 1, *[3 dc in next ch- sp, ch 1] to corner ch-2 sp, (3 dc, ch 2, 3 dc) in corner sp, ch 1, repeat from * to last sp, 3 dc in same sp as beginning ch-3, ch 1. Join round with sc in 3rd ch of the beginning ch-3. [4 ch-1 sps added, one on each side]

rounds 5–8: Repeat Round 4.

round 9: Repeat Round 4. For small block, fasten off.

rounds 10–18 [Large block only]: Repeat Round 4. Fasten off.

Break yarn, leaving a 5" [12.5 cm] tail for weaving in.

Make a total of 4 small Solid Square Blocks and 1 large Solid Square Block.

half square triangle block

With C2 ch 4, Sl st in first ch to form a ring.

round 1 (RS): Ch 3 (counts as 1 dc throughout), 2 dc into ring, [ch 2, 3 dc into ring, ch 2] 3 times. Join round with a Sl st in 3rd ch of beginning ch-3. Fasten off.

round 2 (RS): With RS facing, join C1 with a Sl st in any corner ch-2 sp. Ch 3, 2 dc in same ch-2 sp, ch 1, (3 dc, ch 2, 3 dc) in next ch-2 sp, ch 1, 3 dc in next ch-2 sp, ch 2; drop ch from hook, leaving a long live loop (it will be fastened off at the end of the round). Join C3 with a Sl st in same ch-2 sp, ch 3, 2 dc in same ch-2 sp, ch 1, (3 dc, ch 2, 3 dc) in next ch-2 sp, ch 1, 3 dc in same sp as beginning C1 ch-3, ch 2. With C3 join round with a Sl st in 3rd ch of the beginning C1 ch-3. Fasten off. Return to live stitch on opposite corner and with C1 join round with a Sl st in 3rd ch of beginning C3 ch-3. Fasten off.

round 3: With RS facing, join C1 with a Sl st in two-color ch-2 corner sp with C1 on the left and C3 on the right. Ch 3, 2 dc in same ch-2 sp, ch 1, 3 dc in next ch-1 sp, ch 1, (3 dc, ch 2, 3 dc) in next ch-2 sp, ch 1, 3 dc in next ch-1 sp, ch 1, 3 dc in next corner sp, ch 2; drop ch from hook, leaving a long live loop. Join C3 with a Sl st in same ch-2 sp. ch 3, 2 dc in same sp, ch 1, 3 dc in next ch-1 sp, ch 1, (3 dc, ch 2, 3 dc) in next ch-2 sp, ch 1, 3 dc in next ch-1 sp, ch 1, 3 dc in same sp as beginning C1 ch-3. With C3 join round with a Sl st in 3rd ch of the beginning C1 ch-3. Fasten off. Return to live stitch on opposite corner and with C1 join round with a Sl st in 3rd ch of beginning C3 ch-3. Fasten off. [4 ch-2 corner sps and 8 ch-1 sps]

round 4: With RS facing, join C1 with a Sl st in ch-2 corner sp with C1 on the left and C3 on the right. Ch 3, 2 dc in same ch-2 sp, ch 1, [3 dc in next ch-1 sp, ch 1] to corner sp, (3 dc, ch 2, 3 dc) in corner sp, ch 1, [3 dc in next ch-1 sp, ch 1] to next corner, 3 dc in corner sp, ch 2; drop ch from hook, leaving a live loop (it will be fastened off at the end of the round.) Join C3 with a Sl st in same sp. ch 3, 2 dc in same sp, ch 1, [3 dc in next ch-1 sp, ch 1] to next corner sp, (3 dc, ch 2, 3 dc) in next corner sp, ch 1, [3 dc in next ch-1 sp, ch 1] to beginning corner sp, 3 dc in same sp as the beginning C1 ch-3, ch 2. With C3 join round with a Sl st in

3rd ch of beginning C1 ch-3. Fasten off. Return to live stitch on opposite corner and with C1 join round with a Sl st in 3rd ch of beginning C3 ch-3. Fasten off. [4 ch-1 sps added, one on each side]

rounds 5-9: Repeat Round 4.

Make a total of 8 half square triangle blocks.

assembly

For a polished finish, wet-block individual blocks to target dimensions (see Special Techniques on page 182).

Sew the completed motifs together using Mattress Stitch for Crochet (see Special Techniques on page 186), following the diagram(s) given. Steam seams flat and weave in remaining ends.

finishing
border
note: On Round 1 of the border, you may have to place 2 dcs instead of 3 dcs on either side of the joining seams when they are encountered, to accommodate the wider space created by the seam. This should keep the border fabric from flaring from too many stitches.

round 1 (RS): With RS facing, join C1 with a Sl st in any ch-2 corner sp. Ch 3, 2 dc in same sp, ch 1, *[3 dc in next sp, ch 1] to corner sp, (3 dc, ch 2, 3 dc) in corner sp, ch 1, repeat from * to last sp, 3 dc in same sp as beginning ch-3, ch 1. Join round with sc in 3rd ch of beginning ch-3.

round 2: Ch 3, 2 dc in same sp (around the sc), ch 1, *[3 dc in next sp, ch 1] to corner ch-2 sp, (3 dc, ch 2, 3 dc) in corner sp, ch 1, repeat from * to last sp, 3 dc in same sp as beginning ch-3, ch 1. Join round with sc in 3rd ch of beginning ch-3.

rounds 3-10: Repeat Round 2.

rounds 11 and 12: Repeat Rounds 1 and 2 with C4.

rounds 13: Repeat Round 1 with C2.

rounds 14 and 15: Repeat Round 2 with C2.

Using a tapestry needle, weave in remaining ends. Steam-block border or wet-block entire blanket again.

ASSEMBLY DIAGRAM

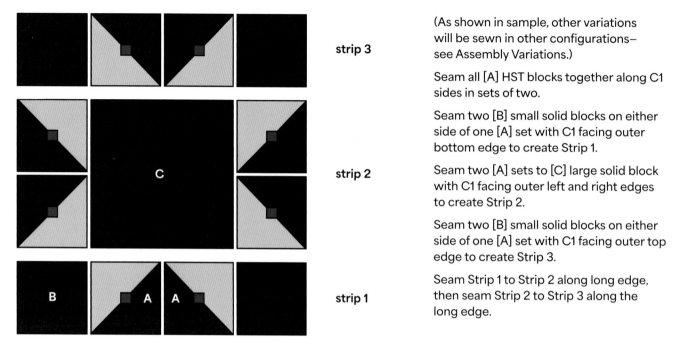

strip 3

strip 2

strip 1

(As shown in sample, other variations will be sewn in other configurations— see Assembly Variations.)

Seam all [A] HST blocks together along C1 sides in sets of two.

Seam two [B] small solid blocks on either side of one [A] set with C1 facing outer bottom edge to create Strip 1.

Seam two [A] sets to [C] large solid block with C1 facing outer left and right edges to create Strip 2.

Seam two [B] small solid blocks on either side of one [A] set with C1 facing outer top edge to create Strip 3.

Seam Strip 1 to Strip 2 along long edge, then seam Strip 2 to Strip 3 along the long edge.

ASSEMBLY VARIATIONS

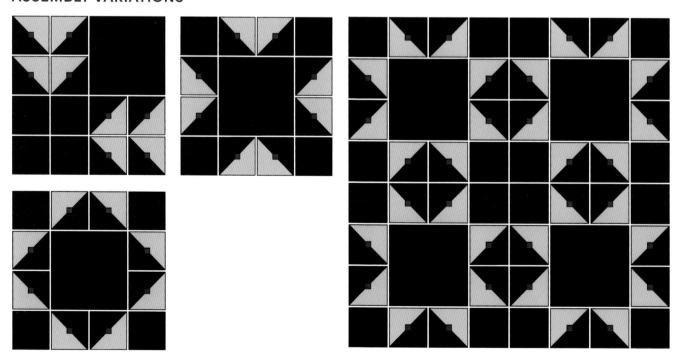

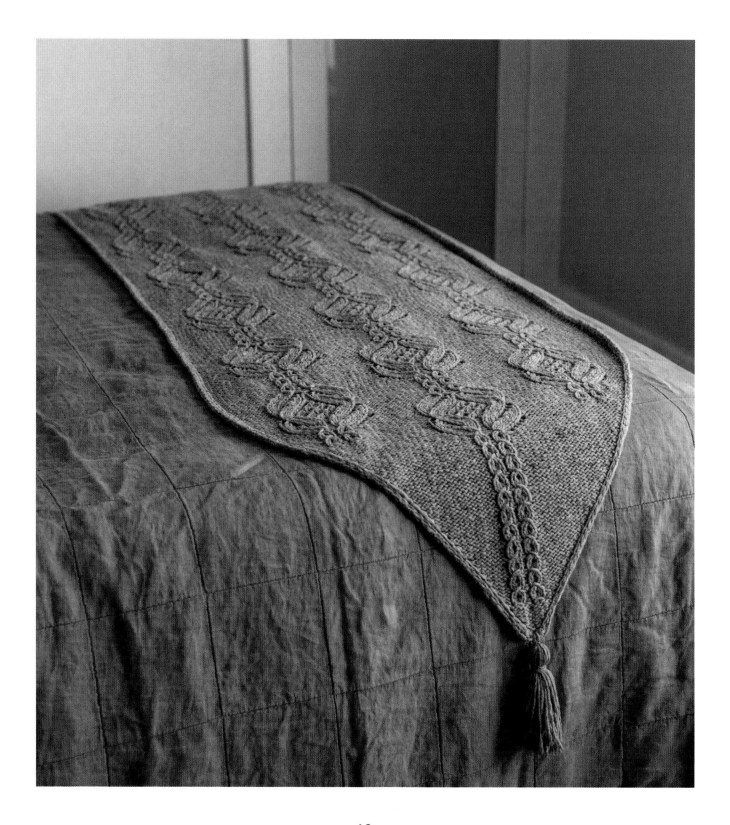

winterly

designed by Pauliina Leisti

A warm woolen bed runner is a beautiful way to finish your layered winter bedding setup, but this decorative blanket does double duty as a wearable shoulder wrap for chilly mornings at home. Lozenge-shaped ends create an elegant overall shape, and a central lace motif flows out from each end to fill the negative space, giving the fabric a timeless feel. The columnar lace panel can be easily lengthened or shortened, making a tailor-made customization for any bed easy. A built-in I-cord edging and voluminous tassels at each end lend a sense of sophistication and polish, while the use of a chunky-weight yarn makes for quick knitting that delivers both warmth and style to your space.

yardage table

blanket size	yardage required	
	yards	meters
bed runner	1378	1260

skill level

●●●○○
Intermediate

finished sizes

bed runner
- W: 26½" × L: 78¼"
- W: 67.5 cm × L: 199 cm

notes

- Length does not include tassels.
- The bed runner's length can be adjusted by adding or subtracting 28-row vertical repeats of Winterly Pattern; each 28-row repeat will add or subtract approximately 5½" [14 cm].
- Adjusting the bed runner's size will affect the total yardage requirements for the project.

PATTERN SPECS

yarn

Chunky-weight wool yarn Bed Runner size shown in Brooklyn Tweed Quarry (200 yards/100 g) in color "Pumice"

gauge

13¼ stitches & 20¼ rows = 4" [10 cm] in blocked Winterly Pattern

needles

One 32" [80 cm] circular needle in size needed to obtain gauge
- Suggested size: US 10½/6.5 mm

notions and tools

- Size US K-10½/6.5 mm crochet hook and smooth waste yarn (for Provisional Crochet Cast-On)
- Spare needle in any style
- Blunt tapestry needle

special techniques

- Provisional Crochet Cast-On: page 186
- Reading Charts: page 186
- Grafting: page 183
- Blocking: page 182

PATTERN INSTRUCTIONS

With waste yarn, cast on 3 stitches using the Provisional Crochet Cast-On (see Special Techniques on page 186).

Switch to working yarn.

Knit 1 row.

*row 1 (RS): Knit 3; slide these 3 stitches back to L needle, pulling the working yarn behind the stitches.

Repeat from * 3 more times, forming an I-cord.

next row (RS): Knit 1-tbl, knit into the back loop of the second stitch on the L needle but do not slip it off L needle, slip the 2nd stitch purlwise WYIB, slip both stitches off L needle at once. Don't turn the work; slide the stitches to the opposite end of the needle.

next row (RS): Slip 1 WYIB, slip 1 WYIF, knit 1-tbl, pick up and knit 3 stitches along left edge of I-cord; unzip the provisional cast-on and place the 3 stitches onto a spare needle, making sure the stitches are in the proper orientation; work knit 1, slip 1 WYIF, purl 1-tbl across these 3 stitches; turn; you now have 9 stitches on your needle.

increase section

Work Rows 1–83 of Increase Pattern (from chart on pages 52–53 or written instructions in Digital Appendix) one time. [91 stitches on your needle]

main fabric

Work Rows 1–38 of Winterly Pattern (from chart below or written instructions in Digital Appendix) 6 times.

decrease section

Work Rows 1–85 of Decrease Pattern (from chart on pages 54–55 or written instructions in Digital Appendix) one time. [9 stitches remain]

next row (WS): Slip 1, purl 2, knit 3, purl 3.

bind-off row (RS): Slip 1, knit 1, k2tog-tbl; slip these 3 stitches back to L needle; knit 2, k2tog-tbl; slip these 3 stitches back to L needle; knit 2, k2tog-tbl. [3 stitches remain on each needle]

Break yarn, leaving an 11" [30 cm] tail. Join stitches using Grafting (see Special Techniques on page 183), holding L needle in front. Secure the BO by going through a couple of edge-stitch loops.

WINTERLY CHART

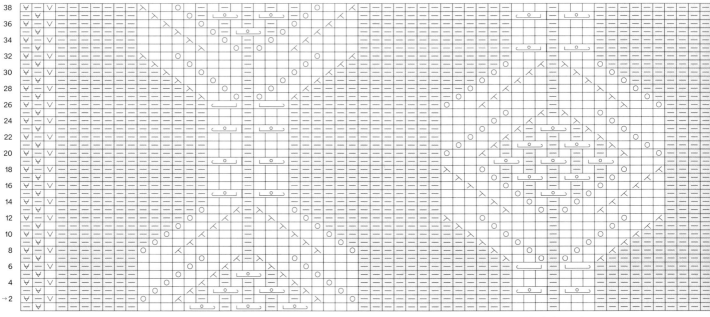

91-stitch panel

finishing

Weave in ends invisibly on the WS. For a polished finish, steam- or wet-block (see Special Techniques on page 182) the blanket to the finished dimensions to set the fabric.

tassels

Make two 6" [15 cm] tassels as follows.

Wrap the yarn approximately 30 times around a book that measures 6" [15 cm]. Break yarn and set aside.

Cut 2 lengths of yarn approximately 10" [25.5 cm] each. Thread both yarns through a large tapestry needle, then fold in half lengthwise with the tapestry needle at the midpoint. Thread the tapestry needle (with tie attached) underneath the wraps of yarn and tie in a knot to secure wraps.

Carefully cut the wraps at the end opposite the tie.

Attach the tassels at each end of the throw by bringing the tassel tails through the center of the tip from opposite sides 2 times. Twist the yarn tails 2 times around the top of the tassel, then thread the yarn tails through the tassel. Trim the tassel ends.

Take a new length of yarn approximately 30" [76 cm] long and wrap it around the tassel several times, ½" [13 mm] below the top. Wrap until the tassel strands are secure. Tie a few knots in the yarn to keep it in place, then wrap the yarn around the tassel again to hide the knots; take the yarn under the wraps to the inside of the tassel and trim ends to measure the same length as the tassel.

INCREASE CHART

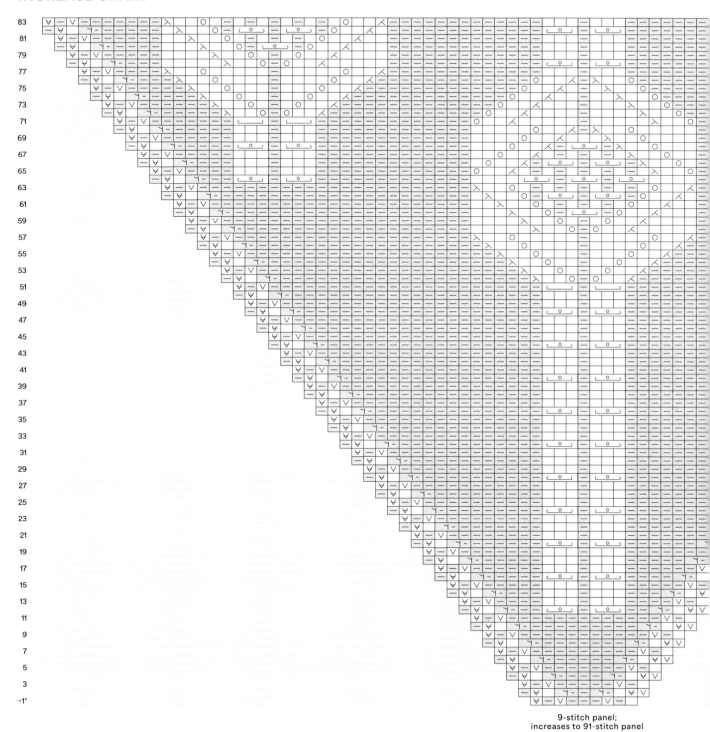

9-stitch panel;
increases to 91-stitch panel

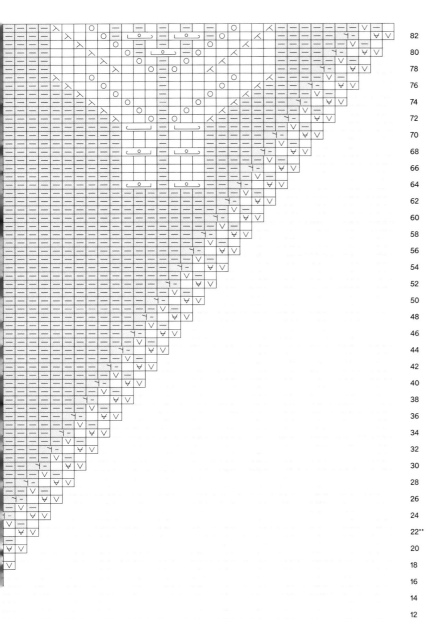

82
80
78
76
74
72
70
68
66
64
62
60
58
56
54
52
50
48
46
44
42
40
38
36
34
32
30
28
26
24
22**
20
18
16
14
12
10
8
6
4
2←

*Note that Row 1 is a WS row.

** A PFB is worked into the fourth stitch of this row. The symbol may be difficult to see, as it crosses the book's binding.

DECREASE CHART

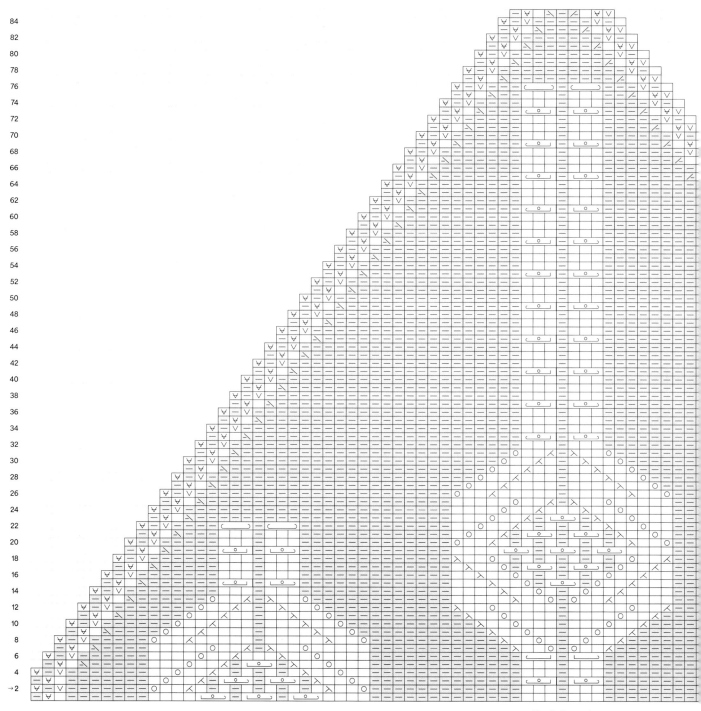

84
82
80
78
76
74
72
70
68
66
64
62
60
58
56
54
52
50
48
46
44
42
40
38
36
34
32
30
28
26
24
22
20
18
16
14
12
10
8
6
4
→2

91-stitch panel;
decreases to 9-stitch panel

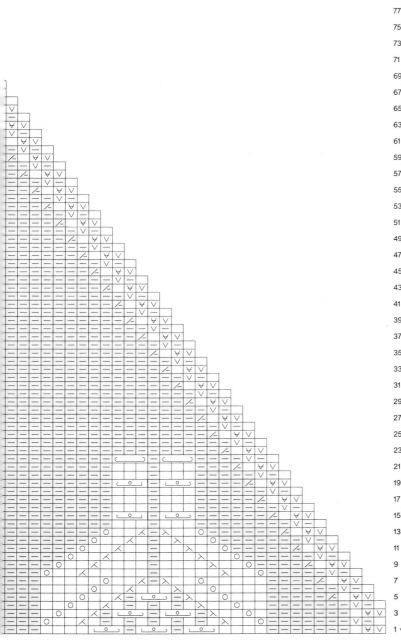

SYMBOL LEGEND

Knit
Knit stitch on RS; purl stitch on WS

Purl
Purl stitch on RS; knit stitch on WS

Slip
On RS slip 1 stitch purlwise with yarn in back;
on WS slip 1 stitch purlwise with yarn in front

Slip WYIF
On RS slip 1 stitch purlwise with yarn in front;
on WS slip 1 stitch purlwise with yarn in back

YO
With yarn in front, bring yarn over top of R needle from
front to back, creating a yarn over (1 stitch increased)

PFB
Purl into the front and then into the back of the
same stitch (1 stitch increased)

K2tog
On RS knit 2 stitches together; on WS purl
2 stitches together (1 stitch decreased; leans right)

SSK
On RS slip 1 stitch knitwise from L to R needle, replace
stitch on L needle in new orientation then knit two stitches
together through the back loops; on WS slip 2 stitches
knitwise one at a time from L to R needle, return these
stitches to L needle in their new orientation and purl them
together through their back loops (1 stitch decreased;
leans left)

P2tog
On RS purl 2 stitches together; on WS knit 2 stitches
together (1 stitch decreased; leans right)

SSP
On RS slip 2 stitches knitwise one at a time from L to
R needle, replace stitches on L needle in new orientation
then purl 2 stitches together through the back loops
(1 stitch decreased; leans left)

Yarn Over Wrap - Left
WYIB slip 1 stitch purlwise from L needle to R needle,
knit 1, YO, knit 1, pass slipped stitch over first 3 stitches
and off R needle

Yarn Over Wrap - Right
Insert tip of R needle into third stitch on L needle, lift it
over the first 2 stitches and off L needle; knit 1, YO, knit 1

Wrap 3 - Left
WYIB slip 3 stitches purlwise from L needle to R needle,
bring yarn to front, slip the same 3 stitches back to
L needle, purl 3

Wrap 3 - Right
Purl 3, WYIB slip the same 3 stitches back to L needle,
bring yarn to back, slip the same 3 stitches back to R needle

Wrap 3
Purl 3, bring yarn to back, slip the same 3 stitches back to
L needle, bring yarn to front, slip the same 3 stitches back
to R needle

rattan

designed by Rastus Hsu

Rattan weaving–traditionally used to create practical, decorative furniture for the home–has remained wildly popular as an interior design element for decades, combining strong geometric shapes with the spirit of handweaving and basketry. This blanket translates the tradition into the medium of wool and pays tribute to this iconic form of woven sculpture.

By cleverly combining the humblest of stitches (knits, purls, and slips) with simple knitted twists, the fabric creates the appearance of woven layers. Strong diagonal lines are imposed over a softer grid of vertical and horizontal lines, resulting in a modern geometric print that will be at home in a wide variety of interiors.

yardage table

blanket size	yardage required	
	yards	meters
stroller	821	751
lap blanket	1349	1234
small throw	2171	1985
large throw	3190	2917
queen bed	6417	5868

skill level

●●○○○
Adventurous Beginner

finished sizes

stroller blanket
• W: 32" × L: 34¾"
• W: 81.5 cm × L: 88.5 cm

lap blanket
• W: 36" × L: 50¾"
• W: 91.5 cm × L: 129 cm

small throw
• W: 48" × L: 61¼"
• W: 122 cm × L: 155.5 cm

large throw
• W: 60" × L: 72"
• W: 152.5 cm × L: 183 cm

queen bed
• W: 88" × L: 98¾"
• W: 223.5 cm × L: 251 cm

special techniques

• Reading Charts: page 186
• Blocking: page 182

PATTERN SPECS

yarn

• Chunky-weight wool yarn
• Small Throw size shown in Brooklyn Tweed Quarry (200 yards/100 g) in color "Lapis"

gauge

14 stitches & 21 rows = 4" [10 cm] in blocked Rattan Pattern

needles

One 40" [100 cm] or longer circular needle in size needed to obtain gauge
• Suggested size: US 11/8 mm

notions and tools

• Cable needle
• Blunt tapestry needle
• T-pins and blocking wires (optional)

PATTERN INSTRUCTIONS

Cast on 112 (126, 168, 210, 308) stitches using your preferred method. For this pattern, we recommend the Long-Tail Cast-On.

tip: If casting on using the Long-Tail method, you can avoid running out of yarn by beginning with two skeins of yarn and tying their ends together to create the initial slipknot. If you have a center-pull yarn ball, you can use both ends of the same ball instead. Break the second strand of yarn after all stitches have been cast on.

bottom edge

Work Rows 1–6 of Bottom Edge Pattern (from chart on opposite page or written instructions in Digital Appendix) one time.

main fabric

Work Rows 1–28 of Rattan Pattern (from chart on opposite page or written instructions in Digital Appendix) 6 (9, 11, 13, 18) times.

top edge

Work Rows 1–8 of Top Edge Pattern (from chart on opposite page or written instructions in Digital Appendix) 1 time.

Bind off all stitches with a relaxed tension.

finishing

Weave in ends invisibly on the WS. For a polished finish, steam- or wet-block (see Special Techniques on page 182) the blanket to the finished dimensions for your chosen size to set the fabric.

TOP EDGE CHART

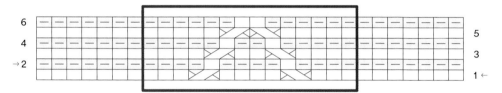

14-stitch repeat

SYMBOL LEGEND

☐ **Knit**
Knit stitch on RS;
purl stitch on WS

□ **Purl**
Purl stitch on RS;
knit stitch on WS

⊻ **Slip WYIF**
Slip 1 stitch purlwise
with yarn in front

⊠ **1/1 LC - Left Cross**
Slip 1 stitch to CN and
hold in front, knit
1 stitch from L needle,
knit stitch from CN

⊠ **1/1 RC - Right Cross**
Slip 1 stitch to CN and
hold in back, knit
1 stitch from L needle,
knit stitch from CN

☐ **Repeat**
Stitches within brackets
create the pattern repeat

RATTAN CHART

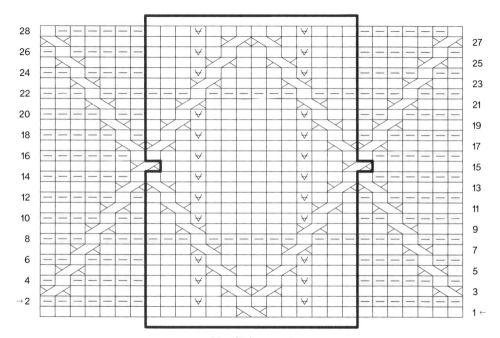

14-stitch repeat

BOTTOM EDGE CHART

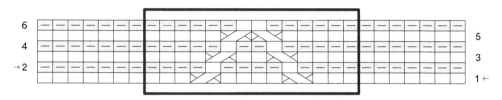

14-stitch repeat

homewood

designed by Seth Richardson

This lusciously cabled blanket is lighter than you might expect thanks to a combination of clever stitch pattern development and yarn choice. The Homewood cable—named after the grove of trees behind the designer's home—balances sinewy, organic cables with large areas of negative space to create a modern, geometric arrangement of traditional cables that feels airy and elegant. The ribbed bands at the bottom and top edges flow unbroken into the cabled fabric and also establish clean side borders that keep the edges of the blanket from curling. Worked in a lofty, woolen-spun yarn at a chunky gauge, the fabric is surprisingly light and airy while still having the sturdy, substantial presence of a classic fisherman's sweater.

yardage table

blanket size	yardage required	
	yards	meters
lap blanket	1301	1190
small throw	2209	2020
large throw	3360	3072
twin bed	4943	4520

skill level

●●○○○
Adventurous Beginner

finished sizes

lap blanket
- W: 33" × L: 47"
- W: 84 cm × L: 119.5 cm

small throw
- W: 45" × L: 58½"
- W: 114.5 cm × L: 148.5 cm

large throw
- W: 57" × L: 70¼"
- W: 145 cm × L: 178.5 cm

twin bed
- W: 63" × L: 93½"
- W: 160 cm × L: 237.5 cm

special techniques
- Reading Charts: page 186
- Blocking: page 182

PATTERN SPECS

yarn
- Chunky-weight wool yarn
- Large Throw size shown in Brooklyn Tweed Quarry (200 yards/100 g) in color "Citrine"

gauge
16 stitches & 22 rows = 4" [10 cm] in blocked Homewood Pattern

needles
One 60" [150 cm] circular needle in size needed to obtain gauge
- Suggested size: US 10/6 mm

notions and tools
- Cable needle
- Blunt tapestry needle
- T-pins and blocking wires (optional)

PATTERN INSTRUCTIONS

Cast on 132 (180, 228, 252) stitches using your preferred method. For this pattern, we recommend the Long-Tail Cast-On.

tip: If casting on using the Long-Tail method, you can avoid running out of yarn by beginning with two skeins of yarn and tying their ends together to create the initial slipknot. If you have a center-pull yarn ball, you can use both ends of the same ball instead. Break the second strand of yarn after all stitches have been cast on.

ribbing

setup row (WS): Slip 2 WYIF, *purl 2, knit 1; repeat from * to last 4 stitches, purl 2, slip 2 WYIF.

row 1 (RS): Knit 4, purl 1, *knit 2, purl 1; repeat from * to last 4 stitches, knit 4.

row 2: Slip 2 WYIF, *purl 2, knit 1; repeat from * to last 4 stitches, purl 2, slip 2 WYIF.

Repeat Rows 1 and 2 five more times, then repeat Row 1 one time, for a total of 14 rows.

main fabric

setup row (WS): Slip 2 WYIF, [purl 2, knit 1] 2 times, [purl 2, knit 16, purl 2, knit 4] 4 (6, 8, 9) times, purl 2, knit 16, [purl 2, knit 1] 2 times, purl 2, slip 2 WYIF.

next row (RS): Knit 4, purl 1, knit 2, purl 1, [knit 2, purl 16, knit 2, purl 4] 5 (6, 8, 9) times, knit 2, purl 16, [knit 2, purl 1] 2 times, knit 4.

next row: Repeat Setup Row.

Work Rows 1–64 of Homewood Pattern (from chart on pages 64–65 or written instructions in Digital Appendix) a total of 3 (4, 5, 7) times, then work Rows 1–38 one more time.

next row (RS): Knit 4, purl 1, knit 2, purl 1, [knit 2, purl 16, knit 2, purl 4] 3 (5, 7, 8) times, knit 2, purl 16, [knit 2, purl 1] 2 times, knit 4.

ribbing

setup row (WS): Slip 2 WYIF, *purl 2, knit 1; repeat from * to last 4 stitches, purl 2, slip 2 WYIF.

row 1 (RS): Knit 4, purl 1, *knit 2, purl 1; repeat from * to last 4 stitches, knit 4.

row 2: Repeat Setup Row.

Repeat Rows 1 and 2 five more times, then repeat Row 1 one more time, for a total of 14 rows.

Bind off all stitches in pattern with a relaxed tension.

finishing

Weave in ends invisibly on the WS. For a polished finish, steam- or wet-block (see Special Techniques on page 182) the blanket to the finished dimensions for your chosen size to set the fabric.

HOMEWOOD CHART

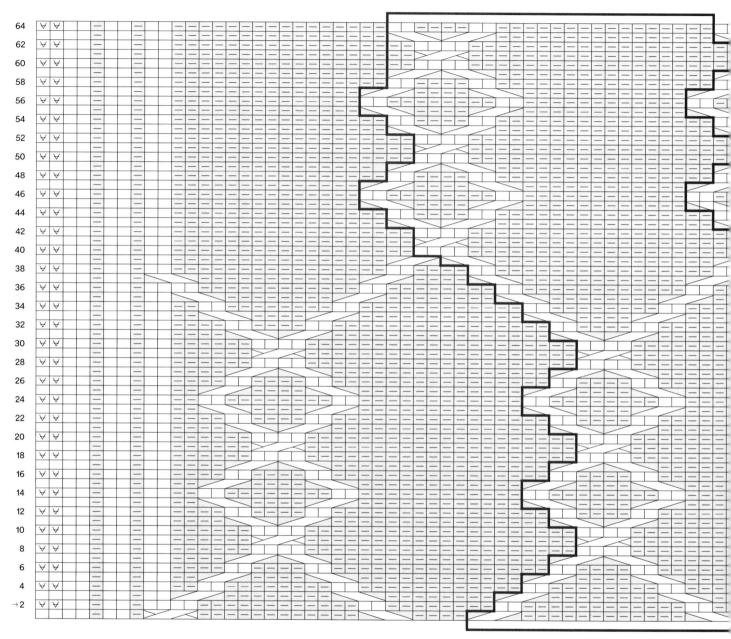

24-stitch repeat

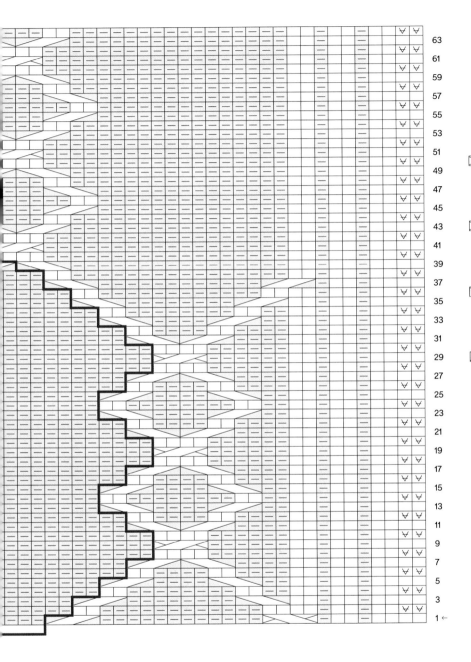

Knit
Knit stitch

Purl
Purl stitch

Slip WYIF
Slip 1 stitch purlwise
with yarn in front

2/2 LC (Left Cross)
Slip 2 stitches to CN and hold
in front, knit 2 stitches from
L needle, knit 2 stitches from CN

2/2 RC (Right Cross)
Slip 2 stitches to CN and hold in
back, knit 2 stitches from
L needle, knit 2 stitches from CN

2/2 LCp (Left Cross over purl)
Slip 2 stitches to CN and hold in
front, purl 2 stitches from
L needle, knit 2 stitches from CN

2/2 RCp (Right Cross over purl)
Slip 2 stitches to CN and hold in
back, knit 2 stitches from
L needle, purl 2 stitches from CN

Repeat
Stitches within brackets create
the pattern repeat

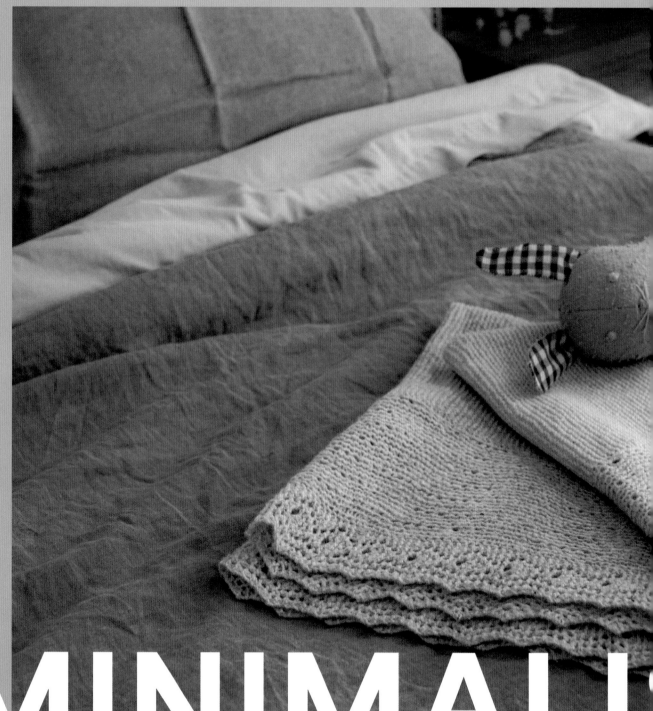

MINIMALI

02

SM

The designs in this chapter are envisioned for spaces that emanate quiet and calm. Though soft and subtle, these pieces are far from boring and layer effortlessly into the calm oases of more minimalistic interiors.

Sophisticated geometric textures and lines are explored here with a controlled range of muted colors. For these patterns, choose smoothly spun yarns in serene, neutral tones.

tessellate 71

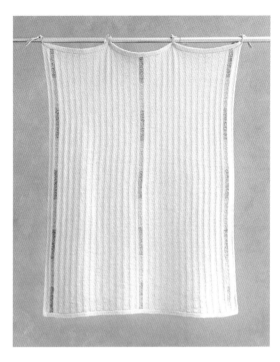

fineline 77

warp + weft 83

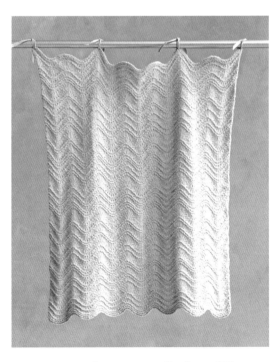

sandstone + shale 87

quill 93

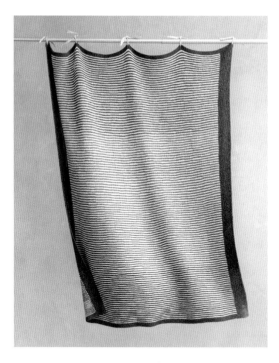

shadowgrid 99

pasqu 103

rainfall 109

tessellate

designed by Ainur Berkimbayeva

This is a beautiful example of how the simplest of stitches can be used to create something truly special. Conceived as an approachable project for beginners, the entire blanket is worked with nothing more than knit and purl stitches. The fabric's vertical ribs and horizontal welts come together like puzzle pieces to create a tessellated pattern of rhythmic textural diamonds. The blanket's architectural lines catch the light and create satisfying texture.

skill level

●○○○○
Beginner

finished sizes

lap blanket
- W: 36¾" × L: 50¼"
- W: 93.5 cm × L: 127.5 cm

small throw
- W: 47" × L: 64¼"
- W: 119.5 cm × L: 163 cm

large throw
- W: 62½" × L: 73¼"
- W: 159 cm × L: 186 cm

special techniques
- Reading Charts: page 186
- Blocking: page 182

yardage table

blanket size	yardage required	
	yards	meters
lap blanket	1797	1643
small throw	2938	2687
large throw	4454	4073

PATTERN SPECS

yarn
- DK-weight wool yarn
- Small Throw size shown in Brooklyn Tweed Arbor (145 yards/50 g) in color "Norway"

gauge
25 stitches & 32 rows = 4" [10 cm] in blocked 2×2 Rib Pattern

needles
One 32" [80 cm] or longer circular needle in size needed to obtain gauge
- Suggested size: US 5/ 3.75 mm

notions and tools
- Stitch markers
- Blunt tapestry needle
- T-pins and blocking wires (optional)

pattern notes
- All the odd-numbered rows are RS rows and even-numbered rows are WS rows throughout.
- To simplify the pattern instructions, work the stitches as they appear on all WS rows, except for 2 outermost selvedge stitches on each side, which are worked in garter stitch (knit the first and last stitch on every row) throughout.

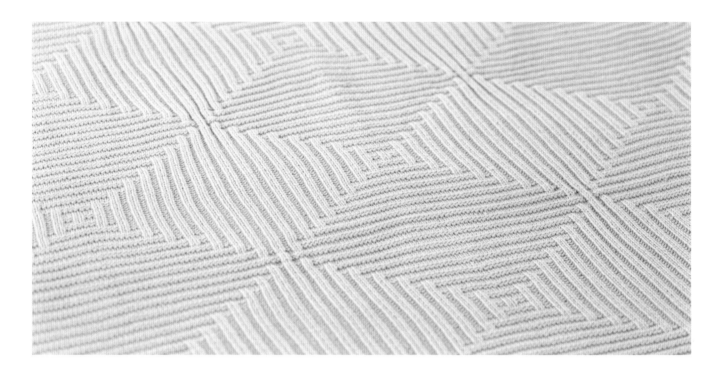

PATTERN INSTRUCTIONS

Cast on 230 (294, 390) stitches using your preferred method. For this pattern, we recommend the Long-Tail Cast-On, but any cast-on will work.

tip: If casting on using the Long-Tail method, you can avoid running out of yarn by beginning with two skeins of yarn and tying their ends together to create the initial slipknot. If you have a center-pull yarn ball, you can use both ends of the same ball instead. Break the second strand of yarn after all stitches have been cast on.

bottom edging

Next 3 rows: Knit to end of row.

setup row (WS): [Knit 2, pm] 2 times, [knit 56 (72, 64), pm] 4 (4, 6) times, knit 2.

note: Slip all markers as you encounter them.

main fabric

Work Rows 1-56 (72, 64) of Tessellate Pattern for your size (from charts on pages 73-75 or written instructions in Digital Appendix) 7 (7, 9) times.

top edging

note: Remove markers as you encounter them on next row.

next row (RS): Knit 2, *knit 2, purl 2; repeat from * to last 4 stitches, knit 4.

next row (WS): *Knit 2, purl 2; repeat from * to last 2 stitches, knit 2.

Repeat last 2 rows 1 more time.

next 4 rows: Knit 2, purl to last 2 stitches, knit 2.

Bind off all stitches purlwise with a relaxed tension.

finishing

Weave in ends invisibly on the WS. For a polished finish, steam- or wet-block (see Special Techniques on page 182) the blanket to the finished dimensions for your chosen size to set the fabric.

CHART: Lap Blanket

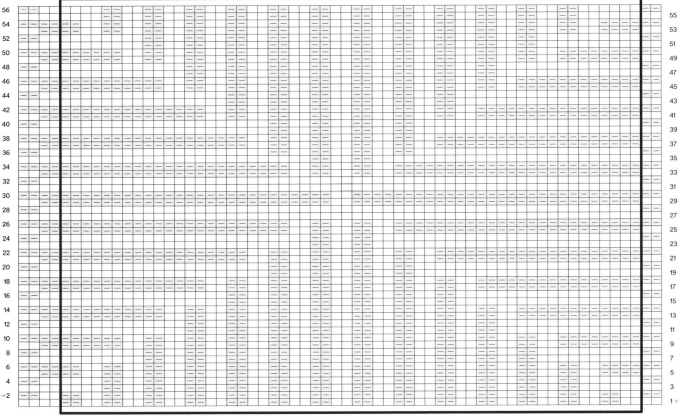

56-stitch repeat

SYMBOL LEGEND

☐ **Knit**
Knit stitch on RS;
purl stitch on WS

⊟ **Purl**
Purl stitch on RS;
knit stitch on WS

▭ **Repeat**
Stitches within
brackets create
the pattern repeat

CHART: Small Throw

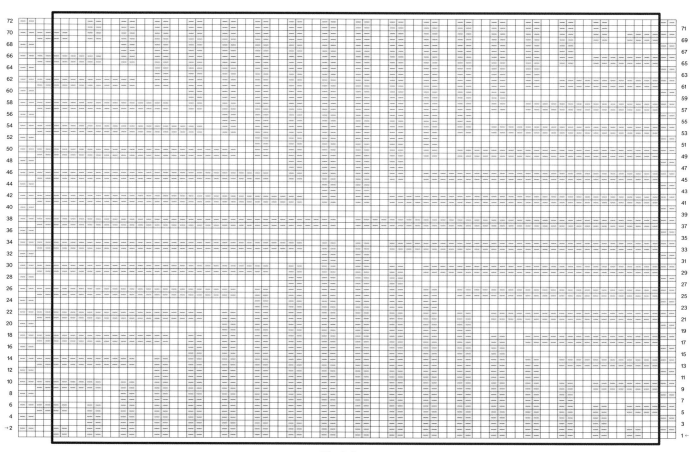

72-stitch repeat

CHART: Large Throw

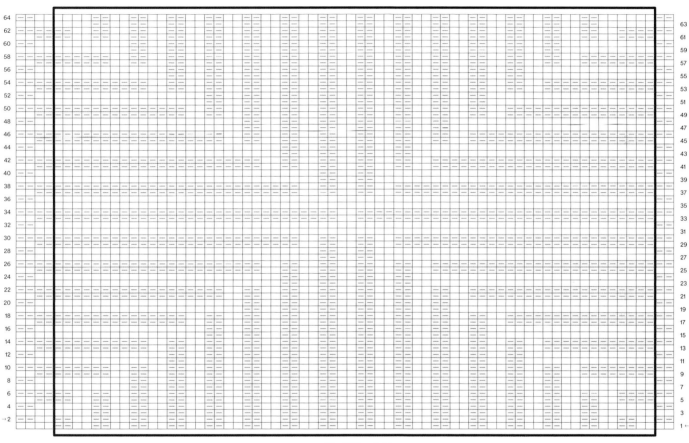

64-stitch repeat

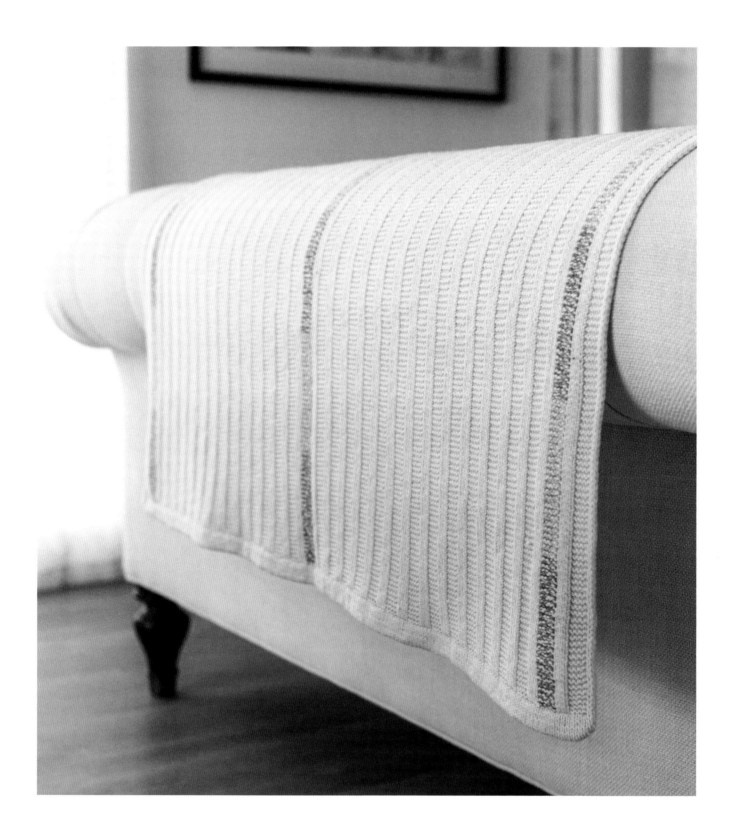

fineline

designed by Stefanie Sichler

This blanket is the perfect project for beginners that want to venture a little further beyond knits and purls. The blanket's thoughtfully placed vertical stripes are created by holding a second strand of contrasting yarn together for some of the garter columns. The version photographed here uses low-contrast tonal color combinations for a poetic, minimalist effect. Bolder contrasts of color and value will play up the linear accents. The blanket features a clean slipped-stitch selvedge along either side, while the top and bottom edges are finished with a polished double hem (with clever corner-shaping details) for added durability and sophistication.

skill level

●●○○○
Adventurous Beginner

finished sizes

lap blanket
• W: 36¾" × L: 48"
• W: 93.5 cm × L: 122 cm

small throw
• W: 48¼" × L: 58"
• W: 122.5 cm × L: 147.5 cm

large throw
• W: 60" × L: 68"
• W: 152.5 cm × L: 172.5 cm

full bed
• W: 90¼" × L: 88"
• W: 229 cm × L: 223.5 cm

special techniques
• Provisional Crochet Cast-On: page 186
• Reading Charts: page 186
• Grafting: page 183
• Blocking: page 182

yardage table

blanket size	C1		C2		C3	
	yards	meters	yards	meters	yards	meters
lap blanket	2138	1955	130	119	98	90
small throw	3753	3432	207	189	155	142
large throw	5472	5004	302	276	226	207
full bed	10652	9740	587	537	440	402

PATTERN SPECS

yarn
• DK-weight wool yarn
• Lap Blanket size shown in Brooklyn Tweed Arbor (145 yards/50 g) in colors "Thaw" (MC), "Arabesque" (C1), and "Degas" (C2)

gauge
24 stitches & 40 rows = 4" [10 cm] in blocked Fineline Pattern with 1 strand of MC

needles
Two 32" [80 cm] or longer circular needles in size needed to obtain gauge
• Suggested size: US 4/ 3.5 mm

notions and tools
• Size US E-4/3.5 mm crochet hook and smooth waste yarn for Provisional Crochet Cast-On
• Blunt tapestry needle
• T-pins and blocking wires (optional)

sizing notes

- The blanket width can be adjusted by adding or subtracting stitches in increments of 7 on either side of the middle stripe, for a total of increments of 14. Each 14-stitch increment adds or subtracts approximately 2¼" [5.5 cm] in width.

- The blanket length can be adjusted as follows:
  + Using 1 accent color: add or subtract one or more 2-row Stripe Pattern repeat(s) (each 2-row repeat adds or subtracts approximately ¼" [6 mm] in height).
  + Using 2 accent colors: add or subtract one or more 2-row Stripe Pattern repeat(s) in each of the 50-row color blocks (each 2-row repeat adds or subtracts approximately ¼" [6 mm] in height); or add or subtract one or more additional 50-row color block(s) (each 50-row color block adds or subtracts approximately 5" [12.5 cm] in height).

- Adjusting the blanket's size will affect the total yardage requirements for the project.

PATTERN INSTRUCTIONS

With waste yarn, cast on 214 (284, 354, 536) stitches using the Provisional Crochet Cast-On (see Special Techniques on page 186).

Switch to working yarn.

Purl 1 row.

bottom border

Work Rows 1–6 of Increase Pattern (from chart on page 81 or written instructions in Digital Appendix). [214 (284, 354, 536) stitches on your needle]

Work Rows 1 and 2 of Transition Pattern (from chart on page 81 or written instructions in Digital Appendix) 4 times.

main fabric

Note: Use a separate ball of contrast color for each of the three knit2y columns. For each 4-stitch knit2y column, knit the 4 stitches with 1 strand each of MC and the indicated contrast color held together. Once the last stitch in the column has been worked, drop the contrast color to the WS and continue in MC only to the next 4-stitch knit2y column.
Do not break contrast color until instructed.

*Work Rows 1 and 2 of Fineline Pattern (from chart on page 81 or written instructions in Digital Appendix) 25 times, using 1 strand each of MC and C1 held together for knit2y columns. Break C1.

Work Rows 1 and 2 of Fineline Pattern 25 times, using 1 strand each of MC and C2 held together for knit2y columns. Break C2.

Repeat from * 4 (5, 6, 8) more times.

Work Rows 1 and 2 of Fineline Pattern 25 times, using 1 strand each of MC and C1 held together for knit2y columns. Break C1.

top border

Work Rows 1 and 2 of Transition Pattern 4 times.

Work Rows 1–6 of Decrease Pattern (from chart on page 81 or written instructions in Digital Appendix).

Knit 1 row (RS). Break MC.

With WS facing, second circular needle, and MC, pick up and knit into each purl bump across the final row of Fineline Pattern (omitting I-cord edge stitches). Use Grafting (see Special Techniques on page 183) to join stitches on spare needle to stitches on working needle.

Unzip the provisional cast-on and place the stitches onto working needle. With WS facing, second circular needle, and MC, pick up and knit into each purl bump across the first row of Fineline Pattern (omitting I-cord edge stitches). Use Grafting to join stitches on spare needle to stitches on working needle.

finishing

Weave in ends invisibly on the WS. For a polished finish, steam- or wet-block (see Special Techniques on page 182) the blanket to the finished dimensions for your chosen size to set the fabric.

INCREASE CHART

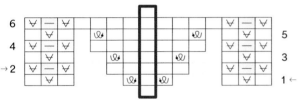

1-stitch repeat

TRANSITION CHART

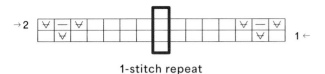

1-stitch repeat

DECREASE CHART

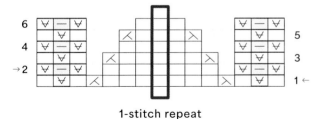

1-stitch repeat

SYMBOL LEGEND

☐ **Knit**
Knit stitch on RS; purl stitch on WS

⊟ **Purl**
Purl stitch on RS; knit stitch on WS

⊻ **Slip WYIF**
Slip 1 stitch purlwise with yarn to RS

⧄ **K2tog**
Knit two stitches from L needle together, creating a right-leaning decrease

⧅ **SSK**
Slip 1 stitch knitwise from L to R needle, replace stitch on L needle in new orientation then knit 2 stitches together through the back loops, creating a left-leaning decrease

⫯ **M1R**
With L needle tip, pick up the running thread between stitch just worked and first stitch on L needle from back to front. Knit the running thread through the front loop (1 stitch increased)

⫯ **M1L**
With L needle tip, pick up the running thread between stitch just worked and first stitch on L needle from front to back. Knit the running thread through the back loop (1 stitch increased)

▨ **Knit2y on RS**
(Knit With 2 Strands of Yarn Held Together)
On RS, knit stitch holding 1 strand each of MC and C1 or C2 together

▨ **Knit2y on WS**
(Knit With 2 Strands of Yarn Held Together)
On WS, knit stitch holding 1 strand each of MC and C1 or C2 together

▭ **Repeat**
Stitches within brackets create the pattern repeat

FINELINE CHART

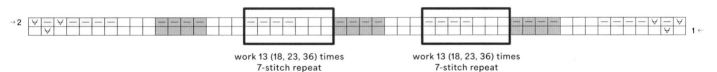

work 13 (18, 23, 36) times
7-stitch repeat

work 13 (18, 23, 36) times
7-stitch repeat

warp + weft

designed by Aistė Butkevičienė

This richly textured blanket combines knits, purls, and strategically placed yarn overs to mimic the appearance of woven fabric at a macro scale. The clever incorporation of fringe—placed on all four sides corresponding to each "woven" strip—furthers the illusion, with a finished piece that appears freshly plucked from a loom. A straightforward and easy-to-work pattern repeat makes this an impactful project that's perfect for beginners. Worked with two strands of fingering weight held double (creating an Aran weight equivalent) allows for further exploration in combining complementary fiber blends or creating homemade marls for unique finished fabrics.

yardage table

blanket size	yardage required	
	yards	meters
lap blanket	3342	3056
crib	4326	3956
small throw	5739	5248
large throw	8535	7804
full bed blanket	14850	13579

PATTERN SPECS

yarn
- Fingering-weight wool yarn, held double (or a single strand of worsted or Aran weight)
- Small Throw size shown in Brooklyn Tweed Loft (275 yards/50 g) in color "Woodsmoke"

gauge
17½ stitches & 26 rows = 4" [10 cm] in blocked Warp + Weft Pattern, with a double strand of yarn

needles
One 32" [80 cm] or longer circular needle in size needed to obtain gauge
- Suggested size: US 8/5 mm

sizing notes
- Fringe is not included in finished dimensions.
- The blanket width can be adjusted by adding or subtracting stitches in increments of 8.
- Length can be adjusted by adding or subtracting rows in increments of 12.
- All custom sizes must begin with the first row of the chart and end with the fourth row of the chart.
- Adjusting the blanket's size will affect the total yardage requirements for the project.

skill level
●●○○○
Adventurous Beginner

finished sizes

lap blanket
- W: 36" × L: 48"
- W: 91.5 cm × L: 121.5 cm

crib blanket
- W: 43¼" × L: 51½"
- W: 110 cm × L: 131 cm

small throw
- W: 48¾" × L: 60½"
- W: 124 cm × L: 154 cm

large throw
- W: 61½" × L: 71½"
- W: 156 cm × L: 181.5 cm

full bed
- W: 85¼" × L: 89½"
- W: 216.5 cm × L: 227.5 cm

special techniques
- Slip-Stitch Selvedge {SSS}: page 187
- Reading Charts: page 186
- Blocking: page 182

notions and tools
- Size US E-4/3.5 mm crochet hook, for fringe
- Blunt tapestry needle
- T-pins and blocking wires (optional)

PATTERN INSTRUCTIONS

With a single strand of yarn, cast on 157 (189, 213, 269, 373) stitches using your preferred method. For this pattern, we recommend the Long-Tail Cast-On.

tip: If casting on using the Long-Tail method, you can avoid running out of yarn by beginning with two skeins of yarn and tying their ends together to create the initial slipknot. Continue to use 2 strands of yarn after all stitches have been cast on.

main fabric

Join second ball of yarn (or continue with both strands if using the Long-Tail Cast-On) to hold yarn double.

Work Rows 1–12 of Warp + Weft Pattern (from chart on opposite page or written instructions in Digital Appendix) 26 (28, 33, 39, 49) times, then work Rows 1–4 one more time. Piece should measure approximately 48½ (52¼, 61½, 72½, 91)" [123 (132.5, 156, 184, 231) cm], ending with Row 4 of pattern.

Break second strand of yarn and continue with a single strand.

Bind off all stitches purlwise with a relaxed tension.

fringe

To prepare the fringe yarn, cut 4" [10 cm] pieces of yarn. You will need to cut up a full skein for the Small Throw size and up to one and a half skeins for the Large Throw and Full Bed sizes. For Lap Blanket and Crib Blanket sizes, you will need approximately three-quarters of a skein.

Take 3 pieces of fringe yarn and fold them in half.

Insert the crochet hook from RS into the first knit stitch one row above the cast-on row and hook the folded yarn loop. Pull the loop through about one-third of the way. Now open up the loop and slip the ends of the yarn (all 6 ends) through the loop. Gently pull it tight to create the first piece of fringe. You may need to adjust the ends as you tighten them to get them all even. Continue adding 3 pieces of fringe yarn to each knit stitch along the cast-on edge, making 3 fringes along every section of knit stitches. Do not work fringes into purl-stitch gaps. Work in the same manner along the bind-off edge of the piece, inserting the hook one row below the bind-off row.

Add fringes to both sides of the piece as described above, working into the 3 gaps between the four purl rows, and inserting the hook into the stitch next to the selvedge stitch (a total of 3 fringes into every section of purl rows). Do not work fringes into the knit-row gaps.

finishing

Do not weave in ends; incorporate them into the closest corner fringes. For a polished finish, steam- or wet-block (see Special Techniques, page 182) the blanket to the finished dimensions for your chosen size to set the fabric. You may want to trim the fringes to all the same length once you've finished, washed, and blocked: Lay the fringe flat, even it out, and trim the ends.

WARP + WEFT CHART

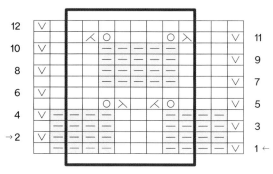

8-stitch repeat

SYMBOL LEGEND

Knit
Knit stitch

Purl
Purl stitch

Slip
Slip 1 stitch purlwise
with yarn to WS

K2tog
Knit two stitches from
L needle together, creating
a right-leaning decrease

SSK
Slip 1 stitch knitwise from L
to R needle, replace stitch on
L needle in new orientation
then knit 2 stitches together
through the back loops, creating a left-leaning decrease

YO
With yarn in front, bring yarn
over top of R needle from
front to back, creating a yarn
over. (1 stitch increased)

Repeat
Stitches within brackets
create the pattern repeat

sandstone + shale

designed by Boann Petersen

This design was born to highlight the beautiful variations of tonally dyed yarns. The undulating fabric is inspired by the classic Old Shale stitch pattern, but with a twist. Just as a jazz performer improvises within the framework of their craft, when you knit this blanket you get to decide where and when to place the wavy purl ridges throughout. Wrong-side rows may be worked as knit or purl rows, creating a texture that enhances the tonal striations of the yarn. For a more traditional look, a solid-color yarn will also work well (see the Baby Blanket version shown on pages 68 and 91). With a wide range of sizes, from crib blanket to king-size coverlet, this textural improvisation will result in a one-of-a-kind piece every time you knit it.

yardage table

blanket size	yardage required	
	yards	meters
cradle	409	374
stroller	859	785
swaddler	1792	1639
lap blanket	1310	1198
small throw	2240	2048
large throw	3315	3031
crib	1690	1545
twin bed	4155	3799
full bed	5815	5317
queen bed	6546	5986
king bed	8515	7786

skill level

●●○○○
Adventurous Beginner

finished sizes

cradle blanket
• W: 18" × L: 30"
• W: 45.5 cm × L: 76 cm

stroller blanket
• W: 31½" × L: 36"
• W: 80 cm × L: 91.5 cm

lap blanket
• W: 36" × L: 48"
• W: 91.5 cm × L: 122 cm

crib blanket
• W: 42¾" × L: 52"
• W: 108.5 cm × L: 132 cm

swaddler
• W: 49¼" × L: 50"
• W: 125 cm × L: 127 cm

small throw
• W: 49¼" × L: 60"
• W: 125 cm × L: 152.5 cm

large throw
• W: 60¾" × L: 72"
• W: 154.5 cm × L: 183 cm

twin bed
• W: 60¾" × L: 90"
• W: 154.5 cm × L: 228.5 cm

full bed
• W: 85¼" × L: 90"
• W: 216.5 cm × L: 228.5 cm

queen bed
• W: 89¾" × L: 96"
• W: 228 cm × L: 244 cm

king bed
• W: 116¾" × L: 96"
• W: 296.5 cm × L: 244 cm

sizing note

Finished lengths after blocking are smaller than lengths listed in the Pattern Table; blocked samples will shrink approximately 10% lengthwise.

special techniques

• Reading Charts: page 186
• Blocking: page 182

PATTERN SPECS

yarn

- DK-weight wool-cotton or wool yarn
- Stroller Blanket size shown in Brooklyn Tweed Dapple (165 yards/50 g) in color "Barely There"
- Queen Bed size shown in Brooklyn Tweed Dapple (165 yards/50 g) in color "Black Walnut"

gauge

- 20½ stitches & 22½ rows = 4" [10 cm] in blocked Sandstone + Shale Pattern A or B
- One 23-stitch pattern repeat measures 4½" [11.5 cm] wide

needles

One 32" [80 cm] or longer circular needle in size needed to obtain gauge
- Suggested size: US 9/ 5.5 mm

notions and tools

- Blunt tapestry needle

pattern notes

- Before casting on, you may want to lay out all of your skeins to assess for color and variation. Rearrange the order of the skeins so the lighter and darker colors work together in the final piece. Or leave it all up to chance and just grab a new skein as you need it!

- The stitch pattern is designed for you to improvise where the purl ridges land. If you want to leave the placement up to chance, you can roll a die for each WS row to determine if the row is knit or purled.

- If you choose to work no purl ridges in the blanket at all, you may wish to cast on 4-6 additional stitches and work a 2- or 3-stitch garter border (knit the first and last 2 or 3 stitches every row) to prevent the edges from curling.

- The pattern is supplied with blank spaces to represent numbers for the different sizes, found in the Pattern Table (opposite). Before knitting the pattern, transfer the numbers for the version you are working from the Pattern Table into the blank spaces provided in the pattern.

PATTERN INSTRUCTIONS

Cast On **A**_____ stitches (from Pattern Table on opposite page) using your preferred method. For this pattern, we recommend the Long-Tail Cast-On.

tip: If casting on using the Long-Tail method, you can avoid running out of yarn by beginning with two skeins of yarn and tying their ends together to create the initial slipknot. If you have a center-pull yarn ball, you can use both ends of the same ball instead. Break the second strand of yarn after all stitches have been cast on.

setup row (WS): Knit to end.

main fabric

Begin main pattern using Sandstone + Shale Pattern A or B (from charts on page 90 or written instructions in Digital Appendix) as noted for your size. Work 4-row repeat until piece measures **B**_____ or desired length, ending with Row 3.

note: The work-to length listed assumes a 10% shrinking of row gauge during blocking.

Bind off all stitches on the next WS row.

finishing

Weave in ends invisibly on the WS. For a polished finish, wet-block (see Special Techniques on page 182) the blanket to the finished dimensions of your chosen size to set the fabric.

PATTERN TABLE

	cradle	stroller	swad-dler	lap	small throw	large throw	crib	twin	full	queen	king
A cast on stitches	92	161	253	184	253	311	219	311	437	460	598
sandstone + shale pattern	A	A	A	A	A	B	B	B	A	A	A
B work-to length, inches	32½	39	52	52	65	78	56½	97¾	97½	104¼	104¼
B work-to length, cm	82.5	99	132	132	165	198	143.5	248.5	248.5	265	265

SANDSTONE + SHALE A CHART

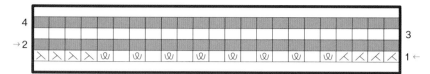

23-stitch repeat

SANDSTONE + SHALE B CHART

23-stitch repeat

SYMBOL LEGEND

Knit
Knit stitch on RS

K2tog
On RS knit 2 stitches together (1 stitch decreased; leans right)

SSK (modified)
On RS slip 1 stitch knitwise from L to R needle, replace stitch on L needle in new orientation then knit two stitches together through the back loops (1 stitch decreased; leans left)

Backward Loop
Make 1 by creating a firm backward loop on R needle (1 stitch increased)

Knit or Purl
On WS rows knit all stitches to create a garter ridge or purl all stitches to create a smooth section

Repeat
Stitches within brackets create the pattern repeat

quill

designed by Jared Flood

This ethereal blanket is an homage to traditional hap shawls of the Shetland islands. These beautiful, utilitarian shawls were made and worn to protect the wearer from the harsh weather conditions of the Scottish Isles. The wavy lace motifs on the broad border of the blanket were often used as a canvas for color experimentation, but haps are equally stunning in a solid color, where natural shades of wool allow the delicate textures to shine. The pattern calls for a lightly spun fingering-weight yarn, but the blanket can be upsized easily using sport, DK, or even worsted weight. Quill is the quintessential heirloom baby blanket, one that I'm proud to say has warmed many babies in the Flood family over the years!

yardage table

blanket size	yardage required	
	yards	meters
swaddler	1100	1006
lap blanket	2150	1996

skill level

●●●○○
Intermediate

finished sizes

swaddler
• 40" square
• 101.5 cm square

lap blanket
• 50" square
• 127 cm square

special techniques

• Provisional Crochet Cast-On: page 186
• Reading Charts: page 186
• Blocking: page 182

PATTERN SPECS

yarn

• Fingering-weight wool yarn
• Swaddler size shown in Brooklyn Tweed Loft (275 yards/50 g) in colors "Fossil" and "Snowbound"

gauge

19 stitches & 38 rows = 4" [10 cm] in blocked garter stitch

needles

One 32" [80 cm] circular needle in size needed to obtain gauge
• Suggested size: US 5/3.75 mm

notions and tools

• Waste yarn and crochet hook for Provisional Crochet Cast-On
• 8 stitch markers, one in a unique appearance for beginning of round
• Blunt tapestry needle
• T-pins and blocking wires (optional)

93

PATTERN INSTRUCTIONS

center square

With waste yarn and crochet hook, cast on 98 (136) stitches using Provisional Crochet Cast-On (see Special Techniques on page 186). Switch to working yarn. Do not join–you will be knitting back and forth.

row 1: Knit all stitches.

row 2: Knit 10, k2tog, knit to end of row. [97 (135) stitches on your needle]

row 3: Knit all stitches.

Repeat the last row, establishing garter stitch, until 97 (135) ridges have been worked on both sides of fabric.

note: One garter stitch ridge is formed for every 2 rows of knitting. For 97 (135) ridges, you will work 194 (270) total rows, not including the waste yarn row from provisional cast-on.

You have now completed your Center Square. You will begin the next blanket section by picking up live stitches from the perimeter of Center Square as follows.

pick-up round: Knit to end of row; do not turn work. Place a marker on R needle, then with working yarn pick up and knit 97 (135) stitches down the side of Center Square (knitting 1 stitch into the space between each garter ridge). Place a second marker on R needle. Carefully unzip the provisional cast-on and place the stitches onto L needle. Knit each of the 97 (135) stitches along provisional edge onto R needle. Place a third marker on R needle. Pick up and knit 97 (135) stitches from remaining side as for previous side. Place fourth and final marker on R needle (we suggest using a marker in a different color to indicate the beginning of round) and join work into the round. [388 (540) stitches–97 (135) for each side of Center Square, with 4 markers placed at each corner]

old shale lace frame

Work Rounds 1-52 (1-55) of Old Shale Pattern (from chart on pages 96-97 or written instructions in Digital Appendix).

chart notes

- Old Shale Chart is repeated 4 times on every round: work 1 instance between each set of corner markers.
- The 19-stitch bracketed motif is repeated 5 (7) times per each instance of Chart worked.
- All rounds are read from right to left.
- Swaddler: Work through Round 52 only; Lap Blanket: Work through Round 55.

Upon completion of the Old Shale Pattern you will have 596 (756) stitches on your needles–149 (189) stitches on each side of square.

lap blanket only

Proceed to Knitted-On Edging section.

swaddler only

next round: *KFB, knit until you reach next marker, sm; repeat from * to the end of round. [4 stitches have been increased; 600 total stitches now on needle]

next round: Purl.

next round: Knit.

knitted-on edging

setup round: Remove beginning-of-round (BOR) marker from current position, purl 2, replace BOR marker, *purl to 1 stitch before next marker. Place a new marker, purl 1, remove old marker, purl 2, replace marker; repeat from * 2 more times. Purl to 3 stitches before BOR marker, place eighth marker, purl 3. Slip BOR marker to R needle.

You now have a section of 3 stitches marked at each corner. These marked stitches indicate the corner turns.

With yarn in back, slip 1 stitch from L to R needle, bring yarn forward, return slipped stitch back to L needle, bring yarn to back. You have just wrapped the first stitch on your L needle, anchoring your working yarn.

Using the Backward Loop Method, cast on 13 (14) stitches onto L needle.

Work Row 1 of Edging Pattern (from chart on page 96 or written instructions in Digital Appendix) over the 13 (14) stitches.

chart notes

- The chart is worked flat: All the odd-numbered rows are RS rows and even-numbered rows are WS rows throughout.
- There is patterning on both RS and WS rows–be sure to review RS and WS instructions within the Legend for all symbols in this chart.
- The last symbol of odd-numbered rows is a "Join" stitch–working the final edging stitch together with the next live blanket perimeter stitch.
- With each repeat of the Edging Pattern, you will consume 6 stitches from the outer perimeter of your blanket.
- Swaddler: Ignore the bracketed stitch in the chart.

Work Rows 2–12 of Edging Pattern.

Repeat Rows 1–12 of Edging Pattern to first set of marked corner stitches.

corner turn

To turn a corner, you will work 12 rows of Edging Pattern (6 edging "joins") as established over three stitches only (the marked corner stitches) as follows.

corner turn: *Work the next RS row of Edging Pattern, working the Join as directed. Work 1 WS row. On the following RS row of Edging Chart, work as directed but replace the Join stitch with a knit stitch. Repeat from * 2 more times, until all marked corner stitches have been consumed. You have just worked 12 rows of Edging Pattern while only consuming 3 perimeter (corner) stitches.

Resume working your knitted-on edging as before, consuming one blanket perimeter stitch for every RS row of edging, to next set of marked corner stitches.** Repeat from ** to ** until all perimeter stitches have been consumed.

Break yarn, leaving a 12" [30.5 cm] tail (leaving these stitches live).

Using a blunt tapestry needle, graft your current row of live/bound-off stitches to the beginning of the edging (the Backward Loop Cast-On). Alternatively, you can bind off the edging stitches, then seam the beginning and end of the edging together.

finishing

Weave in ends invisibly on the WS. Do not cut the woven-in ends until you have blocked your blanket. For a polished finish, wet-block (see Special Techniques on page 182) the blanket to the finished dimensions for your chosen size using T-pins and blocking wires. Let dry completely before unpinning. Remove pins and snip the woven-in ends.

OLD SHALE CHART

EDGING CHART

Swaddler size will cast on one less stitch for Edging than Lap Blanket and will not work stitch shown in the bolded outline. Note that the Edging is worked over a Garter Stitch ground (knit stitches on WS of fabric).

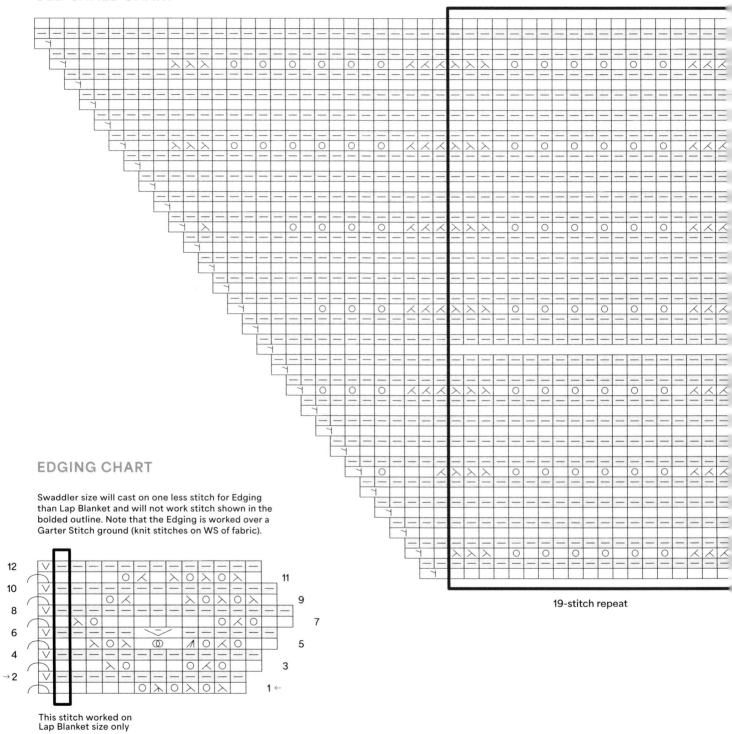

This stitch worked on
Lap Blanket size only

19-stitch repeat

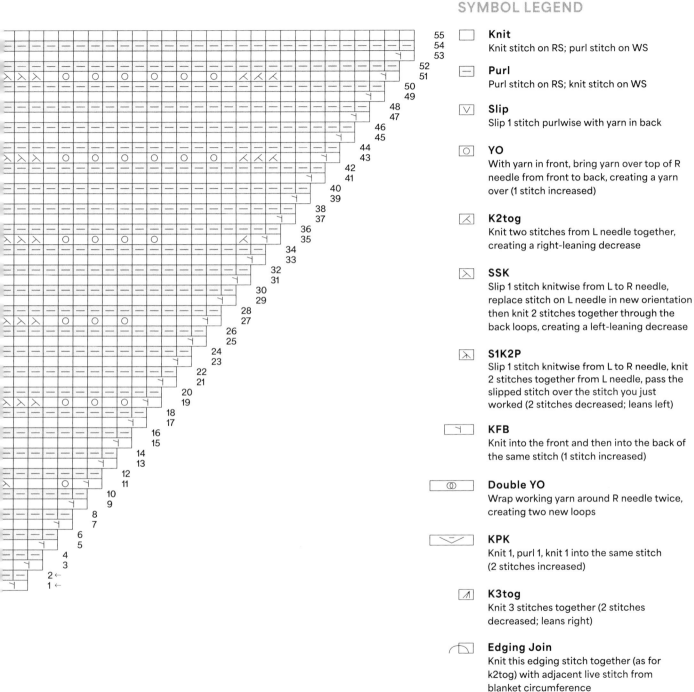

SYMBOL LEGEND

Knit
Knit stitch on RS; purl stitch on WS

Purl
Purl stitch on RS; knit stitch on WS

Slip
Slip 1 stitch purlwise with yarn in back

YO
With yarn in front, bring yarn over top of R needle from front to back, creating a yarn over (1 stitch increased)

K2tog
Knit two stitches from L needle together, creating a right-leaning decrease

SSK
Slip 1 stitch knitwise from L to R needle, replace stitch on L needle in new orientation then knit 2 stitches together through the back loops, creating a left-leaning decrease

S1K2P
Slip 1 stitch knitwise from L to R needle, knit 2 stitches together from L needle, pass the slipped stitch over the stitch you just worked (2 stitches decreased; leans left)

KFB
Knit into the front and then into the back of the same stitch (1 stitch increased)

Double YO
Wrap working yarn around R needle twice, creating two new loops

KPK
Knit 1, purl 1, knit 1 into the same stitch (2 stitches increased)

K3tog
Knit 3 stitches together (2 stitches decreased; leans right)

Edging Join
Knit this edging stitch together (as for k2tog) with adjacent live stitch from blanket circumference

Repeat
Stitches within brackets create the pattern repeat

shadowgrid

designed by Joanna Ignatius

This clever blanket conceals a secret geometry that's hiding in plain sight. Shadow knitting is an ingenious technique, worked with two contrasting colors and a smartly modified form of garter stitch, which creates hidden patterns in fabric that are only visible when viewed from an angle. If you've never seen shadow knitting in person, it really does feel like magic: Look at the fabric straight on, and you'll see a simple black-and-white garter stitch stripe. Angle your view, however, and a checkerboard pattern suddenly appears. Like any good magic trick, this blanket will delight adults and children alike. Shadowgrid reminds us that sometimes a shift in perspective is all we need to appreciate something in a new way.

skill level

●●○○○
Adventurous Beginner

finished sizes

stroller blanket
- W: 30½" × L: 36"
- W: 77.56 cm × L: 91.5 cm

lap blanket
- W: 36½" × L: 48"
- W: 91.5 cm × L: 122 cm

small throw
- W: 48½" × L: 60"
- W: 123 cm × L: 152.5 cm

special techniques

- Reading Charts: page 186
- Blocking: page 182

yardage table

blanket size	main color		contrast color	
	yards	meters	yards	meters
stroller	607	555	433	396
lap blanket	969	886	691	632
small throw	1609	1471	1148	1050

sizing notes

- The blanket width can be adjusted by adding or subtracting stitches in increments of 20. Each 20-stitch increment adds or subtracts approximately 4" [10 cm] in width.
- The blanket length can be adjusted by adding or subtracting 32-row repeats of Shadowgrid Pattern. Each 32-row repeat adds or subtracts approximately 2" [5 cm] in length.
- You can also adjust the blanket width and length by working fewer or more rows of garter stitch on the borders (10 rows of garter stitch is approximately 1" [2.5 cm]).
- Adjusting the blanket's size will affect the total yardage requirements for the project.

PATTERN SPECS

yarn
- DK-weight wool yarn
- Small Throw size shown in Brooklyn Tweed Dapple (165 yards/50 g) in colors "Anchor" (MC) and "Natural" (C1)

gauge
20 stitches & 32 rows = 4" [10 cm] in blocked Shadowgrid Pattern

needles
One 32" [80 cm] or longer circular needle in size needed to obtain gauge
- Suggested size: US 7/ 4.5 mm

notions and tools
- Blunt tapestry needle
- T-pins and blocking wires (optional)

pattern note
When changing colors, make sure that the working yarn is at the front and take care that you don't pull the working yarn too tightly.

stitch pattern
garter stitch with slipped-stitch selvedges
Worked over any number of stitches; 1-row repeat
row 1 (RS): Slip 1 purlwise WYIF, knit to last stitch, slip 1 purlwise WYIF.
Repeat Row 1 for pattern.

PATTERN INSTRUCTIONS

bottom border
With MC, cast on 132 (152, 212) stitches using your preferred method. For this pattern, we recommend the Long-Tail Cast-On.

tip: If casting on using the Long-Tail method, you can avoid running out of yarn by beginning with two skeins of yarn and tying their ends together to create the initial slipknot. If you have a center-pull yarn ball, you can use both ends of the same ball instead. Break the second strand of yarn after all stitches have been cast on.

Knit one row.

Begin Garter Stitch with Slipped-Stitch Selvedges; work until piece measures approximately 1" [2.5 cm].

transition row (WS): Slip 1 purlwise WYIF, knit to last stitch, slip 1 purlwise WYIF.

main fabric
Join C1 and work Rows 1–32 of Shadowgrid Pattern (from chart on opposite page or written instructions in Digital Appendix) 8 (11, 14) times, then work Rows 1–15 one more time.

top border
transition row (WS): Slip 1 purlwise WYIF, *purl 10, knit 10; repeat from * to last 11 stitches, purl 11. Break C1.

Resume Garter Stitch with Slipped-Stitch Selvedges as worked for first border; work for 8 rows, or to the same length as the first border, ending with a WS row.

Bind off all stitches in pattern from RS with a relaxed tension.

right border

With MC and RS facing, pick up and knit 1 stitch from the purl bump of the cast-on edge, pick up and knit 145 (193, 241) stitches from the slipped stitches along the right edge, pick up and knit 1 stitch from the purl bump of the bind-off edge. [147 (195, 243) stitches on your needle]

Begin Garter Stitch with Slipped-Stitch Selvedges; work until border measures 2 (3, 3)" [5 (7.5, 7.5) cm], ending with a WS row.

Bind off all stitches in pattern from RS with a relaxed tension.

left border

With MC and RS facing, pick up and knit 1 stitch from the purl bump of the bind-off edge, pick up and knit 145 (193, 241) stitches from the slipped stitches along the left edge, pick up and knit 1 stitch from the purl bump of the cast-on edge. [147 (195, 243) stitches on your needle]

Begin Garter Stitch with Slipped-Stitch Selvedges; work until border measures 2 (3, 3)" [5 (7.5, 7.5) cm], ending with a WS row.

Bind off all stitches in pattern from RS with a relaxed tension.

finishing

Weave in ends invisibly on the WS. For a polished finish, steam- or wet-block (see Special Techniques on page 182) the blanket to the finished dimensions for your chosen size to set the fabric.

SHADOWGRID CHART

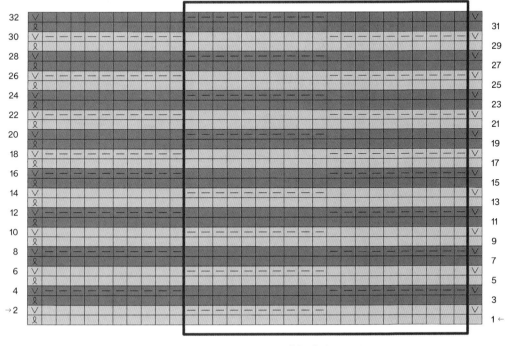

20-stitch repeat

SYMBOL LEGEND

MC
Main Color

C1
Color 1

Knit
Knit stitch on RS;
purl stitch on WS

Purl
Purl stitch on RS;
knit stitch on WS

Knit 1-tbl
Knit stitch through the
back loop, twisting it

Slip WYIF
Slip 1 stitch purlwise
with yarn in front on WS

Repeat
Stitches within brackets
create the pattern repeat

pasqu

designed by Lis Smith

Inspired by knotted wool rugs from Morocco, this blanket reinterprets the traditional crocheted granny square as something bold and unexpected. Working in strongly contrasting black, white, and marled yarns further accentuates the architectural nature of the design, though explorations in color will be equally stunning! The blanket is composed of two larger center diamond blocks, two side half-diamond blocks, and four corner triangle blocks—all are worked individually then seamed together before being finished with a crocheted border that frames the whole. Shown here as a Large Throw in worsted-weight yarn; smaller variations may be achieved by following the pattern as written using fingering- or DK-weight yarn instead.

skill level
●●○○○
Adventurous Beginner

finished size
large throw
- W: 46" × L: 94"
- W: 117 cm × L: 239 cm

individual panel dimensions
- Center Diamonds:
  30" square [76 cm square]
- Large Triangles:
  30 × 30 × 46"
  [76 × 76 × 117 cm]
- Small Triangles:
  22 × 22 × 30"
  [56 × 56 × 76 cm]

yardage table

blanket size	C1		C2		C3	
	yards	meters	yards	meters	yards	meters
large throw	2050	1875	694	635	585	535

special techniques
- Blocking: page 182
- Mattress Stitch for Crochet: page 186

PATTERN SPECS

yarn
- Worsted-weight wool yarn
- Shown in Brooklyn Tweed Shelter (140 yards/50 g) in colors "Cast Iron" (C1), "Fossil" (C2), and "Newsprint" (C3)

gauge
18 stitches & 9 rounds/ rows = 4" [10 cm] in blocked double crochet (US)

hooks
- Main: Suggested size: US 7/4.5 mm or size needed to achieve gauge
- Border: Suggested size: US G-6/4.25 mm or one size smaller than main hook

notions and tools
- Blunt tapestry needle
- T-pins and blocking wires
- Firmly spun sock yarn in a similar color for seaming

PATTERN INSTRUCTIONS

This blanket is made of 8 individually crocheted pieces. The center diamonds are worked in the round with RS facing. The small and large triangles are worked back and forth. After blocking, the pieces are then sewn together. A simple one-round border is worked around the entire blanket once the blocks have been seamed. You may wish to crochet over your ends when possible to cut down on weaving-in during finishing.

block instructions

center diamond

Two Center Diamonds are needed for the blanket layout. Work Rounds 1–25 for the center color blocks in C1, Rounds 26 and 27 in C2, Rounds 28–31 in C3, and Rounds 32 and 33 in C2. When one diamond has been completed, repeat instructions for the second diamond.

Ch 4, Sl st in first ch to form a ring.

round 1 (RS): Ch 3 (counts as 1 dc throughout), 2 dc into ring, [ch 2, 3 dc into ring] 3 times. Join round with sc in 3rd ch of beginning ch-3. (This "joining sc" acts as a ch 1 and leaves the hook in the middle of the resulting space, ready to work the next round.) [4 ch-2 sps]

round 2 (RS): Ch 3, 2 dc in same sp (around the sc), ch 1, [(3 dc, ch 2, 3 dc) in next ch-2 sp, ch 1] 3 times, 3 dc in same sp as beginning ch-3, ch 1. Join round with sc in 3rd ch of the beginning ch-3. [4 ch-2 corner sps; 4 ch-1 sps]

round 3: Ch 3, 2 dc in same sp, ch 1, 3 dc in next ch-sp, ch 1, [(3 dc, ch 2, 3 dc) in next ch-2 sp, ch 1, 3 dc in next ch-1 sp, ch 1] 3 times, 3 dc in same sp as beginning ch-3 , ch 1. Join round with sc in 3rd ch of beginning ch-3. [4 ch-2 corner sps; 8 ch-1 sps]

round 4: Ch 3, 2 dc in same sp, ch 1, *[3 dc in next ch- sp, ch 1] to corner ch-2 sp, (3 dc, ch 2, 3 dc) in corner sp, ch 1, repeat from * to last sp, 3 dc in same sp as beginning ch-3, ch 1. Join round with sc in 3rd ch of beginning ch-3. [4 ch-1 sps added, one on each side]

rounds 5–33: Repeat Round 4.

large triangle

Two Large Triangles are needed for the blanket layout (sides). Work Rows 1–19 for the main color block in C1, Rows 20 and 21 in C2, Rows 22–25 in C3, Rows 26 and 27 in C2, and Rows 28–33 in C1. When one triangle has been completed, repeat instructions for the second triangle.

With C1 and larger hook, ch 5, Sl st in first ch to form a ring.

row 1 (RS): Ch 4 (counts as dc, ch 1 throughout), 3 dc into ring, ch 1, 3 dc into ring, ch 1, dc into ring, turn. [2 3-dc groups, 3 ch-1 sps, 2 dc]

row 2 (WS): Ch 4, 3 dc in first ch-sp, ch 1, (3 dc, ch 2, 3 dc) in center ch-sp, ch 1, 3 dc in last ch-sp, ch 1, dc in 3rd ch of beginning ch-4, turn. [4 3-dc groups, 4 ch-1 sps, 1 ch-2 center sp, 2 dc]

row 3: Ch 4, 3 dc in first sp, ch 1, 3 dc in next sp, ch 1, (3 dc, ch 2, 3 dc) in center sp, ch 1, 3 dc in next sp, ch 1, 3 dc in last sp, ch 1, dc in 3rd ch of beginning ch-4, turn. [6 3-dc groups, 6 ch-1 sps, 1 ch-2 center sp, 2 dc]

row 4: Ch 4, 3 dc in first sp, ch 1, [3 dc in next sp, ch 1] to center sp, (3 dc, ch 2, 3 dc) in center sp, ch 1, [3 dc in next ch-1 sp, ch 1] to last sp, 3 dc in last sp, ch 1, dc in 3rd ch of beginning ch-4, turn. [2 3-dc groups and 2 ch-1 sps added]

rows 5–33: Repeat Row 4.

small triangle

Four Small Triangles are needed for the blanket layout (corners). Work Rows 1–19 for the main color block in C1, Rows 20 and 21 in C2, Rows 22–25 in C3, Rows 26 and 27 in C2, and Rows 28–33 in C1. When one triangle has been completed, repeat instructions for three more triangles.

With C1, ch 5, Sl st in first ch to form a ring.

row 1 (RS): Ch 4 (count as dc, ch 1 throughout), 3 dc into ring, ch 1, dc into ring, turn. [1 3-dc group, 2 ch-1 sps, 2 dc]

row 2 (WS): Ch 4, 3 dc in first ch-sp, ch 1, 3 dc in last ch-sp. ch 1, dc in 3rd ch of beginning ch-4, turn. [2 3-dc groups, 3 ch-1 sps, 2 dc]

row 3: Ch 4, [3 dc in next ch-sp, ch 1] 3 times, dc in 3rd ch of beginning ch-4, turn. [3 3-dc groups, 4 ch-1 sps, 2 dc]

row 4: Ch 4, [3 dc in next ch-sp, ch 1] across, dc in 3rd ch of beginning ch-4, turn.

rows 5–33: Repeat Row 4.

ASSEMBLY DIAGRAM

assembly

For a polished finish, wet-block panels to dimensions (see Special Techniques on page 182).

Sew the completed motifs together as indicated below, using Mattress Stitch for Crochet (see Special Techniques on page 186).

Place Center Diamonds RS up, point to point.

Align the first small triangle with the last worked row facing the top left edge of top Diamond, seam.

Align one large triangle with the last worked row facing into space made by the bottom left edge of top Diamond and the top left edge of bottom square, seam.

Align the second small triangle with the last worked row facing the bottom left edge of bottom Diamond, seam.

Align the third small triangle with the last worked row facing the bottom right edge of bottom Diamond, seam.

Align the second large triangle with the last worked row facing into space made by the bottom right edge of top Diamond and the top right edge of bottom square, seam.

Align the fourth small triangle with the last worked row facing the top right edge of top Diamond, seam.

Steam seams flat and weave in ends on WS of fabric.

border

round 1 (RS): With smaller hook, join C2 with a Sl st in any corner space (the starting ch-5 loop of small triangle), ch 3, 2 dc in same corner sp, *[ch 1, 3 dc in next ch 4 sp] to next ch-5 corner sp, ch 1**, [(3 dc, ch 2, 3 dc) in corner sp, repeat from * around, ending last repeat at **, ch 1, 3 dc in same sp at beginning ch-3, ch 2. Join round with a Sl st in 3rd ch of beginning ch-3.

rainfall

designed by Stefanie Sichler

Rainfall is a beginner-friendly blanket that allows the knitter to focus on the meditative combinations of knits and purls while sharpening the ability to read the knitted fabric as you work–a great skill for any knitter to practice. Inspired by the backdrop of steady rainfall that accompanies life in Oregon, the vertical chains of stockinette diamonds descend a pebbly background of squishy moss stitch. Presented with four sizes, the design is easily customizable by adding or subtracting pattern repeats in easy-to-sub increments. Working with a soft and luxurious merino, you may find that you enjoy the soothing process of making this blanket as much as you'll enjoy snuggling down beneath it when it's complete.

yardage table

blanket size	yardage required	
	yards	meters
lap blanket	1241	1135
small throw	2060	1884
large throw	3168	2897
queen bed	6132	5607

PATTERN SPECS

yarn
- Worsted-weight wool yarn
- Large Throw size shown in Brooklyn Tweed Imbue (104 yards/50 g) in color "Crepe"

gauge
20 stitches & 28 rows = 4" [10 cm] in blocked Moss Stitch

needles
One 32" [80 cm] or longer circular needle in size needed to obtain gauge
- Suggested size: US 7/4.5 mm

One 32" [80 cm] or longer circular needle two sizes smaller than main needle
- Suggested size: US 5/3.75 mm

skill level
●●○○○
Adventurous Beginner

finished sizes

lap blanket
- W: 35½" × L: 47¾"
- W: 90 cm × L: 121.5 cm

small throw
- W: 47½" × L: 59¼"
- W: 120.5 cm × L: 150.5 cm

large throw
- W: 59½" × L: 72¾"
- W: 151 cm × L: 185 cm

queen bed
- W: 87½" × L: 95¾"
- W: 222.5 cm × L: 243 cm

sizing notes
- The blanket width can be adjusted by adding or subtracting stitches in increments of 20.
- Each 20-stitch increment adds or subtracts approximately 4" [10 cm] in width.
- The blanket length can be adjusted by adding or subtracting 16-row repeats of Rainfall Pattern. Each 16-row repeat adds or subtracts approximately 2¼" [5.5 cm] in length.
- Adjusting the blanket's size will affect the total yardage requirements for the project.

special techniques
- Italian Tubular Cast-On: page 184
- Reading Charts: page 186
- Italian Tubular Bind-Off: page 184
- Blocking: page 182

notions and tools
- Blunt tapestry needle
- T-pins and blocking wires (optional)

stitch pattern
moss stitch

Worked over an odd number of stitches; 4-row repeat

row 1 (RS): *Purl 1, knit 1; repeat from * to last stitch, purl 1.

row 2 (WS): *Knit 1, purl 1; repeat from * to last stitch, knit 1.

row 3: Repeat Row 2.

row 4: Repeat Row 1.

Repeat Rows 1–4 for pattern.

PATTERN INSTRUCTIONS

With smaller needle, cast on 177 (237, 297, 437) stitches using your preferred method. For this pattern, we recommend the Italian Tubular Cast-On (see Special Techniques on page 184). Make sure that upon turning the work, you are set up to start with a purl stitch.

bottom border
Work Row 1 of Moss Stitch.

Switch to larger needle.

Work Rows 2–4 of Moss Stitch one time, then work Rows 1–4 one more time.

main fabric
Work Rows 1–14 of Transition A Pattern (from chart on opposite page or written instructions in Digital Appendix) one time.

Work Rows 1–16 of Rainfall Pattern (from chart on opposite page or written instructions in Digital Appendix) 18 (23, 29, 39) times.

Work Rows 1–16 of Transition B Pattern (from chart on opposite page or written instructions in Digital Appendix) one time.

top border
Work Rows 3 and 4 of Moss Stitch one time, Rows 1–4 one time, then Row 1 one more time.

Switch to smaller needle.

Work Row 2 of Moss Stitch.

Bind off all stitches using your preferred method. For this pattern, we recommend the Italian Tubular Bind-Off (see Special Techniques on page 184).

finishing
Weave in ends invisibly on the WS. For a polished finish, steam- or wet-block (see Special Techniques on page 182) the blanket to the finished dimensions for your chosen size to set the fabric.

TRANSITION A CHART

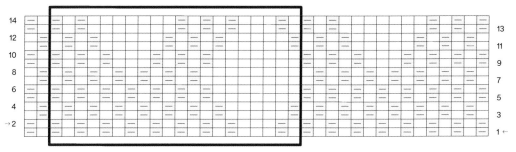

20-stitch repeat

SYMBOL LEGEND

Knit
Knit stitch on RS;
purl stitch on WS

Purl
Purl stitch on RS;
knit stitch on WS

Repeat
Stitches within
brackets create the
pattern repeat

RAINFALL CHART

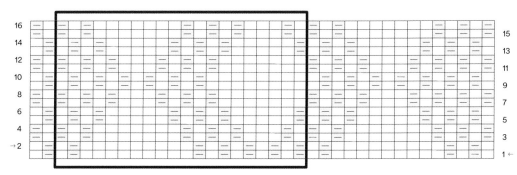

20-stitch repeat

TRANSITION B CHART

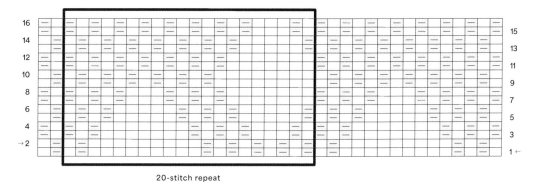

20-stitch repeat

COLORPL

AY

03

Bold, geometric designs explore the intersection of modern art and quilting traditions to create brilliant blankets that truly stand out. These designs provide ideal opportunities for color expression— I think of them as blank canvases, waiting to be transformed into art.

Choose yarns that offer a rich and varied palette of colors in both light and dark values. Tonal color stories create beautiful, painterly variations, while combinations of bright, complementary colors maximize the bold geometry of these artful ideas.

canyonland 117

strata 123

bau 131

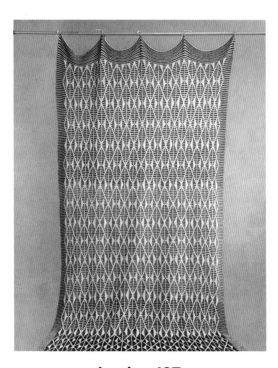

kogin 137

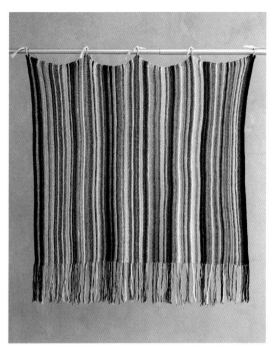

scrappy 143

overlay 147

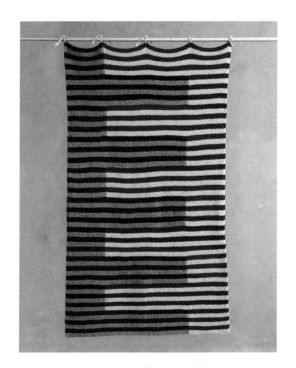

quarterline 153

vitraux 157

canyonland

designed by Aistė Butkevičienė

This striking eight-color blanket is a masterclass in tone blending and texture. A series of short rows creates waves of color and repeating circles reminiscent of traditional paper-pieced quilts. These shapely organic waves are softer than traditional stripes, and their tonal color combinations yield a beautiful optical effect. The pebbly texture of Canyonland will be more (or less) pronounced depending on how much you stretch the fabric when blocking. Purl ridges are worked at the top of each band to highlight the wave forms and add subtle texture throughout. The blanket shown presents a harmonious, warm color story of overdyed yarns. Explore creative color stories of your own to make a one-of-a-kind piece that stimulates your imagination.

skill level
●●●○○
Intermediate

finished sizes

small throw
• W: 52½" × L: 56"
• W: 133.5 cm × L: 143 cm

large throw
• W: 59½" × L: 67"
• W: 151 cm × L: 171 cm

twin bed
• W: 66¾" × L: 78"
• W: 169.5 cm × L: 199 cm

yardage table

blanket size	C1		C2		C3		C4		C5		C6		C7		C8	
	y	m	y	m	y	m	y	m	y	m	y	m	y	m	y	m
small throw	381	348	445	407	368	336	394	360	368	336	394	360	381	348	381	348
large throw	516	472	602	550	499	456	534	488	499	456	534	488	516	472	516	472
twin bed	674	616	786	719	651	595	696	636	651	595	696	636	674	616	674	616

sizing note

Finished dimensions before washing and blocking are significantly smaller than listed above. Prior to blocking, the waves are puffier and have an egg crate-like texture. After blocking, the waves flatten, remaining only slightly textured, and the finished dimensions increase significantly. Blocked samples will enlarge approximately 10% lengthwise and 25-30% widthwise.

special techniques
• Short Rows: Wrap & Turn Method: page 187
• Reading Charts: page 186
• Blocking: page 182

PATTERN SPECS

yarn

- Worsted-weight wool yarn
- Large Throw size shown in Brooklyn Tweed Tones (140 yards/50 g) in colors "Melba Overtone" (C1), "Melba Undertone" (C2), "Goldfinch Overtone" (C3), "Goldfinch Undertone" (C4), "Persimmon Overtone" (C5), "Persimmon Undertone" (C6), "Lychee Overtone" (C7), and "Lychee Undertone" (C8).

gauge

18 stitches = 4" [10 cm] & 48 rows = 5½" [14 cm] in blocked Canyonland Pattern

note: Row gauge should be measured from the lowest point of a wave on Row 1 to the lowest point of a wave in the same column on Row 12.

needles

One 32" [80 cm] or longer circular needle in size needed to obtain gauge

- Suggested size: US 7/4.5 mm

notions and tools

- Blunt tapestry needle
- T-pins and blocking wires (optional)

PATTERN INSTRUCTIONS

With C2, cast on 236 (268, 300) stitches using your pre-ferred method. For this pattern, we recommend the Long-Tail Cast-On.

tip: If casting on using the Long-Tail method, you can avoid running out of yarn by beginning with two skeins of yarn and tying their ends together to create the initial slipknot. If you have a center-pull yarn ball, you can use both ends of the same ball instead. Break the second strand of yarn after all stitches have been cast on.

bottom border

Begin working garter stitch (knit every row). Work even for 10 rows, ending with a WS row.

note: Do not break nonworking yarn when changing color unless indicated. At the beginning of each follow-ing RS row, carry nonworking yarn up the WS, twisting it with working yarn right after the selvedge on WS. At the beginning of each new stripe, check nonworking yarn to control yarn tension along the edge. Join in each new color as needed.

main fabric

*With C1, work Rows 1-6 of Canyonland Pattern (from chart on pages 120-121 or written instructions in Digital Appendix).

With C2, work Rows 7-12 of Canyonland Pattern.*

Repeat from * to * 2 (3, 4) more times.

With C1, work Rows 1-6 of Canyonland Pattern.

With C4, work Rows 7-12 of Canyonland Pattern.

Repeat from * to * 1 more time. Break C1.

With C3, work Rows 1-6 of Canyonland Pattern.

With C2, work Rows 7-12 of Canyonland Pattern. Break C2.

**With C3, work Rows 1-6 of Canyonland Pattern.

With C4, work Rows 7-12 of Canyonland Pattern.**

Repeat from ** to ** 1 (2, 3) more time(s).

With C3, work Rows 1-6 of Canyonland Pattern.

With C6, work Rows 7-12 of Canyonland Pattern.

Repeat from ** to ** 1 more time. Break C3.

With C5, work Rows 1-6 of Canyonland Pattern.

With C4, work Rows 7-12 of Canyonland Pattern. Break C4.

***With C5, work Rows 1-6 of Canyonland Pattern.

With C6, work Rows 7-12 of Canyonland Pattern.***

Repeat from *** to *** 1 (2, 3) more time(s).

With C5, work Rows 1-6 of Canyonland Pattern.

With C8, work Rows 7-12 of Canyonland Pattern.

Repeat from *** to *** 1 more time. Break C5.

With C7, work Rows 1-6 of Canyonland Pattern.

With C6, work Rows 7-12 of Canyonland Pattern. Break C6.

****With C7, work Rows 1-6 of Canyonland Pattern.

With C8, work Rows 7-12 of Canyonland Pattern.****

Repeat from **** to **** 2 (3, 4) more times.

With C7, work Rows 1-6 of Canyonland Pattern. Break C7.

top border

With C8, work 9 rows even in garter stitch, ending with a RS row. Bind off all stitches knitwise with a relaxed tension.

finishing

Weave in ends invisibly on the WS. For a polished finish, steam- or wet-block (see Special Techniques on page 182) the blanket to the finished dimensions for your chosen size to flatten and set the fabric.

CANYONLAND CHART

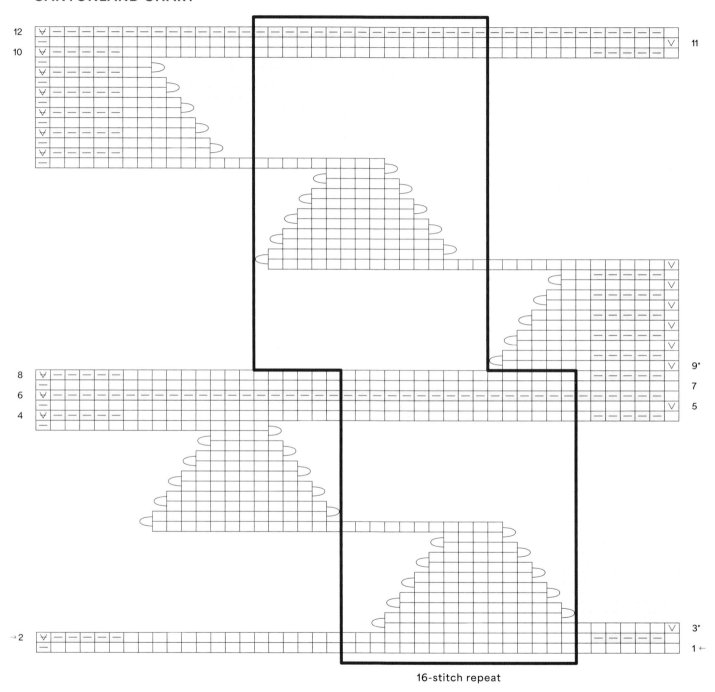

16-stitch repeat

*These sets of short rows correspond to Rows 3 and 9 respectively of the written stitch pattern.

SYMBOL LEGEND

☐ **Knit**
Knit stitch on RS;
purl stitch on WS

⊟ **Purl**
Purl stitch on RS;
knit stitch on WS

⊻ **Slip WYIB**
On RS slip 1 stitch
purlwise with yarn
in back; on WS slip
1 stitch purlwise
with yarn in front

⩔ **Slip WYIF**
On RS slip 1 stitch
purlwise with yarn
in front; on WS slip
1 stitch purlwise
with yarn in back

**Wrap & Turn
(W&T)**
Slip next stitch
from L to R needle,
bring yarn to other
side of work, return
slipped stitch to
L needle; turn work
and proceed to
next row of chart

☐ **Repeat**
Stitches within
brackets create the
pattern repeat

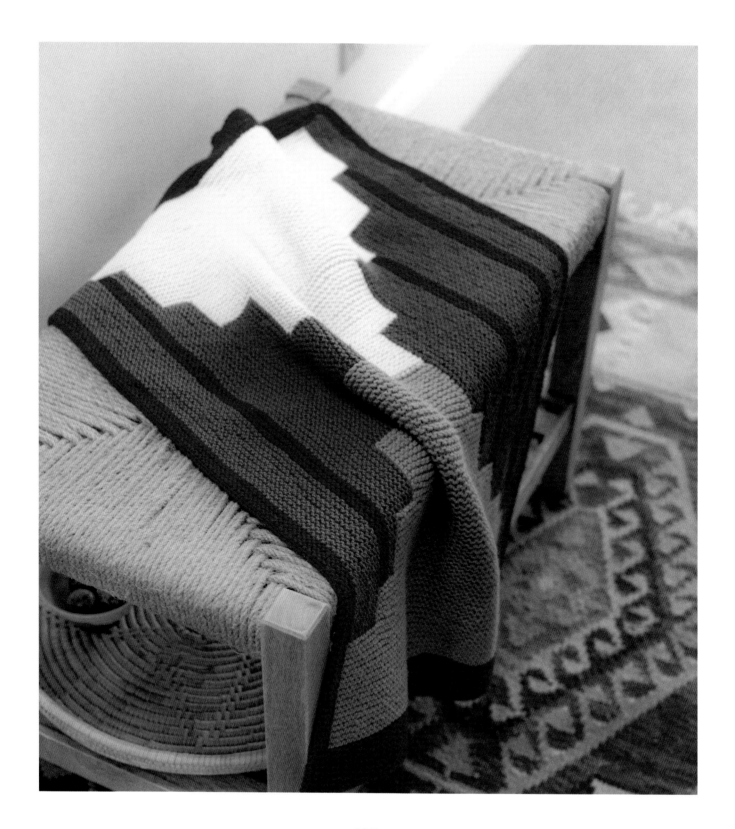

strata

designed by Orlane Sucche

This eye-catching baby blanket reinterprets log cabin knitting via a modern block inspired by the works of modernist painters Helen Frankenthaler and Josef Albers. Rather than following the traditional "puzzle-piece" approach of a log cabin (see the Cabin Quilt on page 169), Strata starts from a central square and builds outward for the entire course of the blanket, creating bold slabs of garter stitch that incorporate color blocking and stripes. Choose color stories inspired by your favorite landscapes or works of modern art. The baby blanket is written as a single size, but it can be enlarged by working with worsted-weight or chunky yarns

skill level

●●○○○
Adventurous Beginner

finished size

cradle blanket
• W: 21¾" × L: 30"
• W: 55 cm × L: 76 cm

special techniques

• Blocking: page 182

yardage table

blanket size	C1		C2		C3		C4		C5	
	y	m	y	m	y	m	y	m	y	m
cradle	173	158	120	110	198	181	122	112	199	182

PATTERN SPECS

yarn

• DK-weight wool yarn
• Shown in Brooklyn Tweed Arbor (145 yards/50 g) in colors "Thaw" (C1), "Mesa" (C2), "Tincture" (C3), "Burnished" (C4), and "Butte" (C5)

gauge

18½ stitches & 37 rows = 4" [10 cm] in blocked garter stitch

needles

One 32" [80 cm] or longer circular needle in size needed to obtain gauge
• Suggested size: US 7/ 4.5 mm

note

Interchangeable circular needles are highly recommended for this project. This allows you to use the cables as stitch holders and save time between blocks.

If using interchangeable circular needles, you will need:
• 2 sets of needle tips (Suggested size: US 7/4.5 mm)
• 5 short cables (10-16" [25-40 cm])
• 5 longer cables (minimum 20" [50 cm])
• 4 pairs of cord stoppers
If you prefer, you may use waste yarn or spare circular needles as stitch holders instead of using interchangeable needle cords.

notions and tools

• Waste yarn or spare circular needles (if not using interchangeable circular needles)
• Blunt tapestry needle
• T-pins and blocking wires (optional)

pattern notes

- This blanket is worked entirely in garter stitch and there is no seaming involved. Work begins with a center segment. A second segment is picked up and knit off of the first, then each successive segment is worked off of two or more previous segments, rotating the blanket clockwise until the entire piece is complete.

- For a neat finish, it is recommended to pick up stitches into the outer bump of edge stitches.

- If using interchangeable needles and cables to hold stitches, begin with short cables. You will change for larger cables as necessary as you work.

- Refer to the construction diagram on page 129 while working the blanket. Each segment begins where the arrow and segment number are located, and is worked in the direction indicated.

PATTERN INSTRUCTIONS

segment 1

With C1, cast on 12 stitches using your preferred method. For this pattern, we recommend the Long-Tail Cast-On.

Begin garter stitch (knit every row): Work 24 rows (12 ridges) in total, ending with a WS row.

Place all stitches on hold by switching the needle tips for cord stoppers if working with interchangeable needles, or by transferring the stitches to a spare needle or waste yarn if working with regular circular needles.

segment 2

Attach needle tips to another cable if necessary.

With RS facing, rotate work 90 degrees to the right (clockwise) so that cast-on edge is on the left. With C2, pick up and knit 12 stitches along the side edge of Segment 1.

Work 23 rows (12 ridges) in garter stitch, ending with a WS row.

Break yarn and place all stitches on hold using your preferred method.

segment 3

Attach needle tips to another cable if necessary. With RS facing, turn work 90 degrees to the right. With C3, pick up and knit 24 stitches along the edges of Segments 2 and 1.

Work 23 rows (12 ridges) in garter stitch, ending with a WS row.

Break yarn and place all stitches on hold using your preferred method.

segment 4

Attach needle tips to another cable if necessary.

With RS facing, turn work 90 degrees to the right. With C4, pick up and knit 24 stitches along the edges of Segments 3 and 2.

Work 11 rows (6 ridges) in garter stitch, ending with a WS row.

Break yarn and place all stitches on hold using your preferred method.

segment 5

With RS facing, turn work 90 degrees to the right. With C1, pick up and knit 6 stitches along the edge of Segment 4; attach a second pair of needle tips to the cable that holds stitches from Segment 1 (or transfer those stitches from waste yarn to spare needle); knit across these 12 stitches, then pick up and knit 12 stitches along the edge of Segment 2; you now have 30 stitches on your needle.

Work 29 rows (15 ridges) in garter stitch, ending with a WS row.

Break yarn and place all stitches on hold using your preferred method.

segment 6

With RS facing, turn work 90 degrees to the right. With C2, pick up and knit 15 stitches along the edge of Segment 5; attach a second pair of needle tips to the cable that holds stitches from Segment 2 (or transfer those stitches from waste yarn to spare needle); knit across these 12 stitches, then pick up and knit 12 stitches along the edge of Segment 3; you now have 39 stitches on your needle.

Work 17 rows (9 ridges) in garter stitch, ending with a WS row.

Break yarn and place all stitches on hold using your preferred method.

segment 7

With RS facing, turn work 90 degrees to the right. With C3, pick up and knit 9 stitches along the edge of Segment 6; attach a second pair of needle tips to the cable that holds stitches from Segment 3 (or transfer those stitches from waste yarn to spare needle); knit across these 24 stitches, then pick up and knit 6 stitches along the edge of Segment 4; you now have 39 stitches on your needle.

Work 23 rows (12 ridges) in garter stitch, ending with a WS row.

Break yarn and place all stitches on hold using your preferred method.

segment 8

With RS facing, turn work 90 degrees to the right. With C4, pick up and knit 12 stitches along the edge of Segment 7; attach a second pair of needle tips to the cable that holds stitches from Segment 4 (or transfer those stitches from waste yarn to spare needle); knit across these 24 stitches, then pick up and knit 15 stitches along the edge of Segment 5; you now have 51 stitches on your needle.

Work 17 rows (9 ridges) in garter stitch, ending with a WS row. Break yarn.

Switch to C5 and work 6 rows (3 ridges) in garter stitch, ending with a WS row.

Break yarn and place all stitches on hold using your preferred method.

segment 9

With RS facing, turn work 90 degrees to the right. With C1, pick up and knit 12 stitches along the edge of Segment 8; attach a second pair of needle tips to the cable that holds stitches from Segment 5 (or transfer those stitches from waste yarn to spare needle); knit across these 30 stitches, then pick up and knit 9 stitches along the edge of Segment 6; you now have 51 stitches on your needle.

Work 17 rows (9 ridges) in garter stitch, ending with a WS row.

Break yarn and place all stitches on hold using your preferred method.

segment 10

With RS facing, turn work 90 degrees to the right. With C2, pick up and knit 9 stitches along the edge of Segment 9; attach a second pair of needle tips to the cable that holds stitches from Segment 6 (or transfer those stitches from waste yarn to spare needle); knit across these 39 stitches, then pick up and knit 12 stitches along the edge of Segment 7; you now have 60 stitches on your needle.

Work 11 rows (6 ridges) in garter stitch, ending with a WS row.

Break yarn and place all stitches on hold using your preferred method.

segment 11

With RS facing, turn work 90 degrees to the right. With C3, pick up and knit 6 stitches along the edge of Segment 10; attach a second pair of needle tips to the cable that holds stitches from Segment 7 (or transfer those stitches from waste yarn to spare needle); knit across these 39 stitches, then pick up and knit 12 stitches along the edge of Segment 8; you now have 57 stitches on needle.

Work 17 rows (9 ridges) in garter stitch, ending with a WS row.

Break yarn and place all stitches on hold using your preferred method.

segment 12

With RS facing, turn work 90 degrees to the right. With C4, pick up and knit 9 stitches along the edge of Segment 11; attach a second pair of needle tips to the cable that holds stitches from Segment 8 (or transfer those stitches from waste yarn to spare needle); knit across these 51 stitches, then pick up and knit 9 stitches along the edge of Segment 9; you now have 69 stitches on your needle.

Work 17 rows (9 ridges) in garter stitch, ending with a WS row.

Break yarn and place all stitches on hold using your preferred method.

segment 13

With RS facing, turn work 90 degrees to the right.
With C1, pick up and knit 9 stitches along the edge of Segment 12; attach a second pair of needle tips to the cable that holds stitches from Segment 9 (or transfer those stitches from waste yarn to spare needle); knit across these 51 stitches, then pick up and knit 6 stitches along the edge of Segment 10; you now have 66 stitches on your needle.

Work 23 rows (12 ridges) in garter stitch, ending with a WS row.

Break yarn and place all stitches on hold using your preferred method.

segment 14

With RS facing, turn work 90 degrees to the right.
With C2, pick up and knit 12 stitches along the edge of Segment 13; attach a second pair of needle tips to the cable that holds stitches from Segment 10 (or transfer those stitches from waste yarn to spare needle); knit across these 60 stitches, then pick up and knit 9 stitches along the edge of Segment 11; you now have 81 stitches on your needle.

Work 5 rows (3 ridges) in garter stitch, ending with a WS row. Break yarn.

Switch to C5 and work 6 rows (3 ridges) in garter stitch, ending with a WS row.

Break yarn and place all stitches on hold using your preferred method.

segment 15

With RS facing, turn work 90 degrees to the right.
With C3, pick up and knit 6 stitches along the edge of Segment 14; attach a second pair of needle tips to the cable that holds stitches from Segment 11 (or transfer those stitches from waste yarn to spare needle); knit across these 57 stitches, then pick up and knit 9 stitches along the edge of Segment 12; you now have 72 stitches on your needle.

Work 11 rows (6 ridges) in garter stitch, ending with a WS row.

Break yarn and place all stitches on hold using your preferred method.

segment 16

With RS facing, turn work 90 degrees to the right.
With C4, pick up and knit 6 stitches along the edge of Segment 15; attach a second pair of needle tips to the cable that holds stitches from Segment 12 (or transfer those stitches from waste yarn to spare needle); knit across these 69 stitches, then pick up and knit 12 stitches along the edge of Segment 13; you now have 87 stitches on your needle.

Work 5 rows (3 ridges) in garter stitch, ending with a WS row. Break yarn.

Switch to C5 and work 6 rows (3 ridges) in garter stitch, ending with a WS row.

Break yarn and place all stitches on hold using your preferred method.

segment 17

With RS facing, turn work 90 degrees to the right.
With C1, pick up and knit 6 stitches along the edge of Segment 16; attach a second pair of needle tips to the cable that holds stitches from Segment 13 (or transfer those stitches from waste yarn to spare needle); knit across these 66 stitches, then pick up and knit 6 stitches along the edge of Segment 14; you now have 78 stitches on your needle.

Work 29 rows (15 ridges) in garter stitch, ending with a WS row.

Break yarn and place all stitches on hold using your preferred method.

segment 18

With RS facing, turn work 90 degrees to the right.
With C2, pick up and knit 15 stitches along the edge of Segment 17; attach a second pair of needle tips to the cable that holds stitches from Segment 14 (or transfer those stitches from waste yarn to spare needle); knit across these 81 stitches, then pick up and knit 6 stitches along the edge of Segment 15; you now have 102 stitches on your needle.

Work 17 rows (9 ridges) in garter stitch, ending with a WS row.

Break yarn and place all stitches on hold using your preferred method.

segment 19

With RS facing, turn work 90 degrees to the right. With C3, pick up and knit 9 stitches along the edge of Segment 18; attach a second pair of needle tips to the cable that holds stitches from Segment 15 (or transfer those stitches from waste yarn to spare needle if necessary); knit across these 72 stitches, then pick up and knit 6 stitches along the edge of Segment 16; you now have 87 stitches on your needle.

Work 35 rows (18 ridges) in garter stitch, ending with a WS row.

Break yarn and place all stitches on hold using your preferred method.

segment 20

With RS facing, turn work 90 degrees to the right. With C4, pick up and knit 18 stitches along the edge of Segment 19; attach a second pair of needle tips to the cable that holds stitches from Segment 16 (or transfer those stitches from waste yarn to spare needle); knit across these 87 stitches, then pick up and knit 15 stitches along the edge of Segment 17; you now have 120 stitches on your needle.

Work 11 rows (6 ridges) in garter stitch, ending with a WS row.

Break yarn and place all stitches on hold using your preferred method.

border segment 1

With RS facing, turn work 90 degrees to the right. With C5, pick up and knit 6 stitches along the edge of Segment 20; attach a second pair of needle tips to the cable that holds stitches from Segment 17 (or transfer those stitches from waste yarn to spare needle). Knit these 78 stitches, then pick up and knit 9 stitches along the edge of Segment 18; you now have 93 stitches on needle.

Work 17 rows (9 ridges) in garter stitch, ending with a WS row.

Bind off with a relaxed tension until 1 stitch remains on R needle. Leave stitch on the needle; do not break yarn.

border segment 2

With RS facing, turn work 90 degrees to the right. Using yarn attached to Border Segment 1, pick up and knit 9 stitches along the edge of Border Segment 1; attach a second pair of needle tips to the cable that holds stitches from Segment 18 (or transfer those stitches from waste yarn to spare needle); knit across these 102 stitches, then pick up and knit 18 stitches along the edge of Segment 19; you now have 130 stitches on your needle.

next row (WS): Knit.

row 1 (RS): Slip 1 stitch purlwise WYIF, bring yarn to back, knit to end.

row 2 (WS): Knit.

Repeat Rows 1 and 2 one more time.

Bind off with a relaxed tension until 1 stitch remains on R needle. Leave stitch on the needle; do not break yarn.

border segment 3

With RS facing, turn work 90 degrees to the right. Using yarn attached to Border Segment 2, pick up and knit 3 stitches along the edge of Border Segment 2; attach a second pair of needle tips to the cable that holds stitches from Segment 19 (or transfer those stitches from waste yarn to spare needle); knit across these 87 stitches, then pick up and knit 6 stitches along the edge of Segment 20; you now have 97 stitches on your needle.

next row (WS): Knit.

row 1 (RS): Slip 1 stitch purlwise WYIF, bring yarn to back, knit to end.

row 2 (WS): Knit.

Repeat Rows 1 and 2 seven more times.

Bind off with a relaxed tension until 1 stitch remains on R needle. Leave stitch on the needle; do not break yarn.

border segment 4

With RS facing, turn work 90 degrees to the right. Using yarn attached to Border Segment 3, pick up and knit 9 stitches along the edge of Border Segment 3; attach a second pair of needle tips to the cable that holds stitches from Segment 20 (or transfer those stitches from waste yarn to spare needle); knit across these 120 stitches, then pick up and knit 9 stitches along the edge of Border Segment 1; you now have 139 stitches on your needle.

next row (WS): Knit.

row 1 (RS): Slip 1 stitch purlwise WYIF, bring yarn to back, knit to end.

row 2 (WS): Slip 1 stitch purlwise WYIF, bring yarn to back, knit to end.

Repeat Rows 1 and 2 one more time.

Bind off all stitches with a relaxed tension.

CONSTRUCTION DIAGRAM

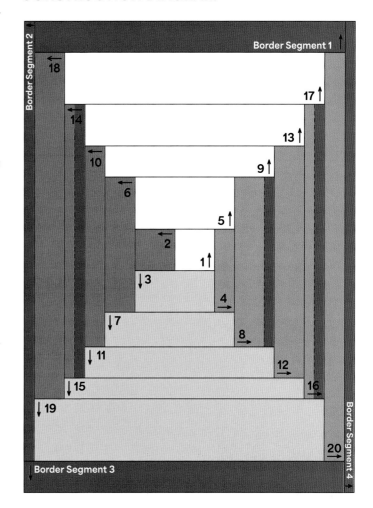

finishing

Weave in ends invisibly on the WS. For a polished finish, steam- or wet-block (see Special Techniques on page 182) the blanket to the finished dimensions to set the fabric.

129

bau

designed by Lis Smith

Two-color garter stitch creates an intriguing textural fabric that's far simpler to work than it looks, thanks to a clever trick with circular needles. The stitch pattern offers room for a dynamic play of color and depth. Bau's graphic blocks are worked using three colors, and the result is a fully reversible fabric. The blanket is worked in three separate panels, end to end, with blocks of different colors alternating along the length of each piece. Once complete, the panels are blocked and seamed, then the blanket is framed with a corded edging (try a bold accent color for an unexpected pop!). Pairing high-contrast colors will enhance the woven look of the stitch pattern as well as the checkerboard motif. Choosing a softer tone-on-tone palette produces a more atmospheric blend with softer transitions.

skill level

●●●○○
Intermediate

finished size

small throw
- W: 46" × L: 53"
- W: 117 cm × L: 134.5 cm

individual panel dimensions
- Left Panel (Narrow):
  W: 12" × L: 60"
  [W: 30.5 cm × L: 152.5 cm]
- Middle Panel (Medium):
  W: 16" × L: 60"
  [W: 40.5 cm × L: 152.5 cm]
- Right Panel (Wide):
  W: 22" × L: 60"
  [W: 56 cm × L: 152.5 cm]

special techniques
- Provisional Crochet Cast-On: page 186
- Grafting: page 183
- Blocking: page 182

yardage table

blanket size	C1		C2		C3		C4	
	yards	meters	yards	meters	yards	meters	yards	meters
small throw	1105	1010	430	393	743	679	74	68

PATTERN SPECS

yarn
- Worsted-weight wool yarn
- Shown in Brooklyn Tweed Tones (140 yards/50 g) in colors "Goldfinch Undertone" (C1), "Zest Overtone" (C2), and "Baseline Overtone" (C3); and Brooklyn Tweed Shelter (140 yards/50 g) in color "Cardinal" (C4)

gauge
18 stitches & 36 rows = 4" [10 cm] in blocked garter stitch

needles
One 32" [80 cm] circular needle in size needed to obtain gauge
- Suggested size: US 8/5 mm
Two DPNs two sizes larger than circular needle
- Suggested size: US 10/6 mm

notions and tools
- Size US H-8/5 mm crochet hook and smooth waste yarn (for Provisional Crochet Cast-On)
- Stitch marker
- Blunt tapestry needle
- T-pins and blocking wires (optional)

stitch pattern

4-row garter stitch

Worked over any number of stitches; 4-row repeat

row 1 (WS): Knit. Do not turn; slide stitches back to opposite end of needle to work another WS row.
Join new yarn on first pass.

row 2 (WS): Purl. Turn.

row 3 (RS): Purl. Do not turn; slide stitches back to opposite end of needle to work another RS row.

row 4 (RS): With yarn indicated in pattern guide, knit. Turn.
Repeat Rows 1–4 for 4-Row Garter Stitch.

pattern notes

- For all panels, when switching colors, be sure to bring the new color up from under the old color to prevent a hole.
- Slip markers as you encounter them.
- The blanket is constructed from three panels worked flat that are seamed when finished to create an abstracted checkerboard.
- The stitch pattern is worked over 4 rows, with 2 WS rows worked before you turn the piece to work 2 RS rows. After working the first WS row, slide stitches back across the circular needle so you are ready to work a WS row again. Turn and work the third row on the RS, then slide stitches back across the circular needle so you are ready to work a RS row again. Turn to begin the stitch pattern again with the first WS row.
- Refer to the Pattern Guide following the Pattern Instructions for Block and Transition Set instructions. Work these sets in the Pattern Order given for each panel.
- A corded border is applied after seaming.

PATTERN INSTRUCTIONS

wide right panel

With waste yarn, cast on 84 stitches using the Provisional Crochet Cast-On (see Special Techniques on page 186). Place marker after stitch 42.
Switch to C1.

pattern order

Work Rows 1–4 of 2-Color A Block 24 times.
Work Rows 1–4 of Transition Set 1 one time.
Work Rows 1–4 of 2-Color B Block 24 times.
Work Rows 1–4 of Transition Set 2 one time.
Work Rows 1–4 of 2-Color A Block 24 times.
Work Rows 1–4 of Transition Set 3 one time.
Work Rows 1–4 of 2-Color C Block 10 times.
Work Rows 1–4 of Transition Set 4 one time.
Work Rows 1–4 of 2-Color D Block 13 times.
Work Rows 1–4 of Transition Set 5 one time.
Work Rows 1–4 of 2-Color C Block 10 times.
Work Rows 1–4 of Transition Set 4 one time.
Work Rows 1–4 of 2-Color D Block 6 times.
Break yarn and transfer stitches to waste yarn.

center medium panel

With waste yarn, cast on 68 stitches using the Provisional Crochet Cast-On. Place marker after stitch 26.
Switch to C2.

pattern order

Work Rows 1–4 of 3-Color A Block 24 times.
Work Rows 1–4 of Transition Set 8 one time.
Work Rows 1–4 of 2-Color E Block 23 times.
Work Rows 1–4 of Transition Set 9 one time.
Work Rows 1–4 of 3-Color A Block 23 times.
Work Rows 1–4 of Transition Set 10 one time.
Work Rows 1–4 of 3-Color B Block 11 times.
Work Rows 1–4 of Transition Set 11 one time.
Work Rows 1–4 of 2-Color F Block 13 times.
Work Rows 1–4 of Transition Set 12 one time.
Work Rows 1–4 of 3-Color B Block 9 times.
Work Rows 1–4 of Transition Set 13 one time.
Join a second ball of C3 and work Rows 1–4 of 2-Color D Block 6 times.
Break yarn and transfer stitches to waste yarn.

left narrow panel

With waste yarn, cast on 54 stitches using the Provisional Crochet Cast-On. Place marker after stitch 27.
Switch to C3.

pattern order

Work Rows 1–4 of 2-Color D Block 24 times.
Work Rows 1–4 of Transition Set 5 one time.
Work Rows 1–4 of 2-Color C Block 23 times.
Work Rows 1–4 of Transition Set 4 one time.
Work Rows 1–4 of 2-Color D Block 23 times.

Work Rows 1-4 of Transition Set 6 one time.
Work Rows 1-4 of 2-Color B Block 10 times.
Work Rows 1-4 of Transition Set 2 one time.
Work Rows 1-4 of 2-Color A Block 13 times.
Work Rows 1-4 of Transition Set 1 one time.
Work Rows 1-4 of 2-Color B Block 10 times.
Work Rows 1-4 of Transition Set 7 one time.
Work Rows 1-4 of 2-Color D Block 6 times.
Break yarn and transfer stitches to waste yarn.

finishing

Weave in ends invisibly on the WS. For a polished finish, wet-block (see Special Techniques on page 182) the panels to the panel dimensions to set the fabric.

Pin the panels together to line up the color change joins (see photo). Sew the side edges of the panels together using C1 and mattress stitch, working panels from left to right: Narrow, Medium, and Wide.

Steam seams flat and weave in remaining ends.

i-cord border

With waste yarn and DPNs, cast on 3 stitches using the Provisional Crochet Cast-On.

Switch to C4.

Knit 3; slide stitches to opposite end of DPN without turning. With RS of blanket facing, beginning at one corner edge and working across long edge first, *knit 2, slip 1 stitch from the L needle to the R needle, pick up a stitch from the blanket edge with the L needle (without knitting it) then return the slipped stitch from the R needle to the L needle. Knit these 2 stitches together through the back loops. Slide your stitches to the opposite end of the needle without turning. Repeat from * around entire piece, picking up approximately 4 stitches for every 6 rows (3 garter ridges) along the long edges, and 1 stitch for each live stitch along the short edges. You may wish to work 1 or 2 plain rows at each corner without picking up, to ease around the corners. Unzip the provisional cast-on and place the live stitches on a spare DPN; join the 2 ends of the border using Grafting (see Special Techniques on page 183). Weave in remaining ends.

PATTERN GUIDE

pattern notes

- rows 1 and 3 of both Block and Transition Sets are all worked with a single color; Rows 2 and 4 are all worked with 2 colors.
- Block Sets create the large color blocks. Transition Sets rearrange the colors (or switch out some of the colors altogether) so they are in the correct positions for the next Block Set.
- You will be instructed to work either to the center of the row, where you'll change colors, or to the end of the row; drop the yarn to the WS when you are done working with it on the current row, but do not break it. You may use the same yarn from the same position (i.e., from the center or at the side edge) on the next pass in the opposite direction, or you may work in separate directions. To minimize the number of tails to weave in later, do not break the yarn until it is clear that you will not need it in the next few rows. Once you have worked through each Block Set once, you will know where you need to break and join colors. Each Transition Set is only worked once; you may wish to break the yarn once you have worked through a Transition Set and begun the next Block Set.
- Slip markers as you come to them.

block sets

2-color A block
row 1 (WS): With C1, knit; slide.

row 2 (WS): With C1, purl to marker, switch to C2 and purl to end; turn.

row 3 (RS): With C1, purl; slide.

row 4 (RS): With C2, knit to marker, switch to C1 and knit to end; turn.

2-color B block
row 1 (WS): With C1, knit; slide.

row 2 (WS): With C2, purl to marker, switch to C1 and purl to end; turn.

row 3 (RS): With C1, purl; slide.

row 4 (RS): With C1, knit to marker, switch to C2 and knit to end; turn.

2-color C block
row 1 (WS): With C3, knit; slide.

row 2 (WS): With C1, purl to marker, switch to C3 and purl to end; turn.

row 3 (RS): With C3, purl; slide.

row 4 (RS): With C3, knit to marker, switch to C1 and knit to end; turn.

2-color D block
row 1 (WS): With C3, knit; slide.

row 2 (WS): With C3, purl to marker, switch to C1 and purl to end; turn.

row 3 (RS): With C3, purl; slide.

row 4 (RS): With C1, knit to marker, switch to C3 and knit to end; turn.

2-color E block
row 1 (WS): With C1, knit; slide.

row 2 (WS): With C3, purl to marker, switch to C1 and purl to end; turn.

row 3 (RS): With C1, purl; slide.

row 4 (RS): With C1, knit to marker, switch to C3 and knit to end; turn.

2-color F block
row 1 (WS): With C1, knit; slide.

row 2 (WS): With C1, purl to marker, switch to C3 and purl to end; turn.

row 3 (RS): With C1, purl; slide.

row 4 (RS): With C3, knit to marker, switch to C1 and knit to end; turn.

3-color A block
row 1 (WS): With C2, knit; slide.

row 2 (WS): With C3, purl to marker, switch to C1 and purl to end; turn.

row 3 (RS): With C2, purl; slide.

row 4 (RS): With C1, knit to marker, switch to C3 and knit to end; turn.

3-color B block
row 1 (WS): With C2, knit; slide.

row 2 (WS): With C1, purl to marker, switch to C3 and purl to end; turn.

row 3 (RS): With C2, purl; slide.

row 4 (RS): With C3, knit to marker, switch to C1 and knit to end; turn.

transition sets

transition set 1
row 1 (WS): With C1, knit; slide.

row 2 (WS): With C2, purl to marker, switch to C1 and purl to end; turn.

row 3 (RS): With C1, purl; slide.

row 4 (RS): With C1, knit to marker, switch to C2 and knit to end; turn.

transition set 2
row 1 (WS): With C1, knit; slide.

row 2 (WS): With C1, purl to marker, switch to C2 and purl to end; turn.

row 3 (RS): With C1, purl; slide.

row 4 (RS): With C2, knit to marker, switch to C1 and knit to end; turn.

transition set 3
row 1 (WS): With C1, knit; slide.

row 2 (WS): With C1, purl to marker, switch to C3 and purl to end; turn.

row 3 (RS): With C3, purl; slide.

row 4 (RS): With C3, knit to marker, switch to C1 and knit to end; turn.

transition set 4
row 1 (WS): With C3, knit; slide.

row 2 (WS): With C3, purl to marker, switch to C1 and purl to end; turn.

row 3 (RS): With C3, purl; slide.

row 4 (RS): With C1, knit to marker, switch to C3 and knit to end; turn.

transition set 5
row 1 (WS): With C3, knit; slide.

row 2 (WS): With C1, purl to marker, switch to C3 and purl to end; turn.

row 3 (RS): With C3, purl; slide.

row 4 (RS): With C3, knit to marker, switch to C1 and knit to end; turn.

transition set 6
row 1 (WS): With C3, knit; slide.

row 2 (WS): With C2, purl with C2, switch to C1 and purl to end; turn.

row 3 (RS): With C1, purl; slide.

row 4 (RS): With C1, knit to marker, switch to C2 and knit to end; turn.

transition set 7
row 1 (WS): With C1, knit; slide.

row 2 (WS): With C3, purl to marker, switch to C1 and purl to end; turn.

transition set 8
row 3 (RS): With C3, purl; slide.

row 4 (RS): With C1, knit to marker, switch to C3 and knit to end; turn.

transition set 8
row 1 (WS): With C2, knit; slide.

row 2 (WS): With C3, purl to marker, switch to C1 and purl to end; turn.

row 3 (RS): With C1, purl; slide.

row 4 (RS): With C1, knit to marker, switch to C3 and knit to end; turn.

transition set 9
row 1 (WS): With C1, knit; slide.

row 2 (WS): With C3, purl to marker, switch to C1 and purl to end; turn.

row 3 (RS): With C2, purl; slide.

row 4 (RS): With C1, knit to marker, switch to C3 and knit to end; turn.

transition set 10
row 1 (WS): With C2, knit; slide.

row 2 (WS): With C3, purl to marker, switch to C1 and purl to end; turn.

row 3 (RS): With C2, purl; slide.

row 4 (RS): With C3, knit to marker, switch to C1 and knit to end; turn.

transition set 11
row 1 (WS): With C1 knit; slide.

row 2 (WS): With C1, purl to marker, switch to C3 and purl to end; turn.

row 3 (RS): With C1, purl; slide.

row 4 (RS): With C3, knit to marker, switch to C1 and knit to end; turn.

transition set 12
row 1 (WS): With C2, knit; slide.

row 2 (WS): With C1, purl to marker, switch to C3 and purl to end; turn.

row 3 (RS): With C2, purl; slide.

row 4 (RS): With C3, knit to marker, switch to C1 and knit to end; turn.

transition set 13
row 1 (WS): With C2, knit; slide.

row 2 (WS): With C1, purl to marker, switch to C3 and purl to end; turn.

row 3 (RS): With C2, purl; slide.

row 4 (RS): With C1, knit to marker, switch to C3 and purl to end; turn.

kogin

designed by Meri Tanaka & Tokuko Ochiai

Traditional Japanese embroidery techniques have been inspiring textile artists for centuries. Kyoto-based designers Meri Tanaka and Tokuko Ochiai used knitting to interpret one such technique, called Kogin, which is traditionally used to add warmth and durability by stitching decorative cotton motifs onto hemp kimonos. Worked in three contrasting colors, a repeating pattern of large slip-stitch diamonds is overlaid on a contrasting ground of garter stitch. Working the main motifs in a white or cream yarn over a backdrop of dark colors highlights the embroidered look while creating bold, textural motifs that will be right at home in modern interiors.

skill level
●●○○○
Adventurous Beginner

finished size
twin bed
• W: 59½" × L: 98"
• W: 151 cm × L: 249.5 cm

special techniques
• Knitted Cast-On: page 185
• Reading Charts: page 186
• Blocking: page 182

yardage table

blanket size	color 1		color 2		color 3	
	yards	meters	yards	meters	yards	meters
twin bed	3408	3116	1584	1448	860	786

PATTERN SPECS

yarn
• DK-weight wool yarn
• Shown in Brooklyn Tweed Arbor (145 yards/50 g) in colors "Thaw" (C1), "Sashiko" (C2), and "Burnished" (C3)

gauge
19 stitches & 40 rows (20 ridges) = 4" [10 cm] in blocked Kogin Pattern

needles
One 40" [100 cm] or longer circular needle in size needed to obtain gauge
• Suggested size: US 7/4.5 mm

notions and tools
• Stitch markers
• Blunt tapestry needle
• T-pins and blocking wires (optional)

pattern note
The chart is shown in two colors, but more than one color may be used in place of the orange C1/C2 symbols. The sample shown alternated between two background color ridges throughout. One, two, or more colors may be used to create the background garter ridges.

PATTERN INSTRUCTIONS

bottom border

note: Break yarn when changing colors.
With MC, cast on 283 stitches using your preferred method. For this pattern, we recommend the Knitted Cast-On (see Special Techniques on page 185).

setup row (WS): Knit.

row 1 (RS): With C1, knit.

row 2 (WS): With C1, knit.

rows 3 and 4: With MC, knit.

rows 5 and 6: With C2, knit.

rows 7 and 8: With MC, knit.

rows 9 and 10: With C1, knit.

rows 11–34: Repeat Rows 3–10 three times.

rows 35–38: Repeat Rows 3–6.

main fabric

note: When changing colors, do not break yarn if color will be used again within 2 rows; carry color not in use up outside edge.

section 1

row 1 (RS): With MC, knit 12, pm, work Row 1 of Kogin Pattern (from chart on page 141 or written instructions in Digital Appendix) to last 12 stitches, pm, knit 12.

row 2 (WS): With MC, knit to marker, sm, work Row 2 of Kogin Pattern to marker, sm, knit to end.

row 3 (RS): With C1, knit to marker, pm, work Row 3 of Kogin Pattern to marker, sm, knit to end.

row 4 (WS): With C1, knit to marker, sm, work Row 4 of Kogin Pattern to marker, sm, knit to end.

Continue in established pattern, knitting first and last 12 stitches of every row, and changing colors every RS row, until you have worked Rows 1–100 of Kogin Pattern a total of 3 times.

Break C1.

section 2

Continuing to work in pattern as established, work Rows 1–100 of Kogin Pattern 3 times, using C2 as background color instead of C1.

Break C2.

section 3

Repeat Section 1.

next row (RS): With MC, knit.

next row (WS): With MC, purl.

top border

note: Break yarn when changing colors.

row 1 (RS): With C3, knit.

row 2 (WS): Knit.

rows 3 and 4: With MC, knit.

rows 5 and 6: With C1, knit.

rows 7 and 8: With MC, knit.

rows 9 and 10: With C2, knit.

rows 11 and 12: with MC, knit.

rows 13–36: Repeat Rows 5–12 three times.

rows 37–40: Repeat Rows 5–8. Break C1 and C2.

Bind off all stitches using MC with a relaxed tension.

finishing

Weave in ends invisibly on the WS. For a polished finish, steam- or wet-block (see Special Techniques on page 182) the blanket to the finished dimensions.

KOGIN CHART

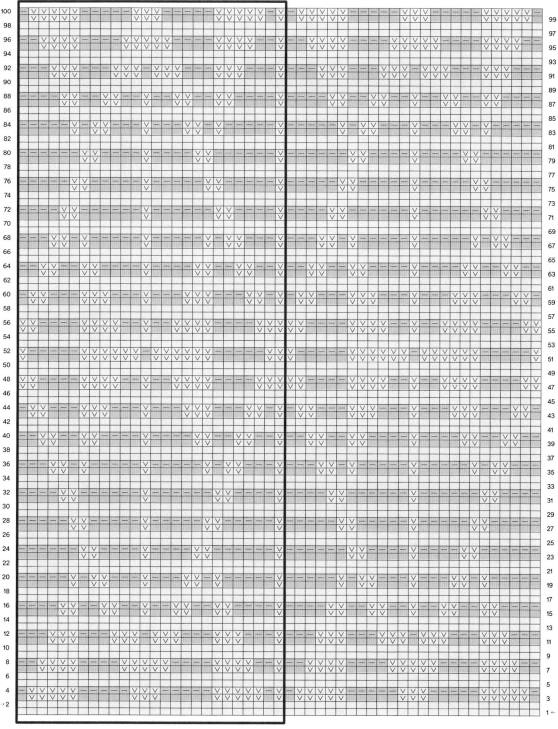

26-stitch repeat

SYMBOL LEGEND

MC
Main Color

C1 or C2
Color 1 or Color 2

Knit
Knit stitch on RS;
purl stitch on WS

Purl
Purl stitch on RS;
knit stitch on WS

Slip
On RS slip 1 stitch
purlwise with yarn
in back; on WS slip
1 stitch purlwise
with yarn in front

Repeat
Stitches within
brackets create the
pattern repeat

scrappy

designed by Hiroka Shinokawa

Here is a creative and beautiful solution for the many small scraps of yarn we crafters accumulate over the years! This simple but creative blanket is not only a great way to employ yarn leftovers, but a fun exercise in combining colors and being spontaneous. The blanket is worked with only knit and purl stitches, and the asymmetrical fringe joyfully eliminates the need to weave in any yarn ends whatsoever! If you're a planner, you can gather all your scraps and sort them by color family before beginning to work, or be spontaneous and grab whatever scraps and colors inspire you in the moment as you work. With this playful design, no two blankets made from the pattern will ever be the same.

skill level

●○○○○
Beginner

yardage table

blanket size	yardage required	
	yards	meters
cradle	397	363
stroller	929	849
swaddler	2007	1835
lap blanket	1495	1367
small throw	2483	2270
large throw	3717	3399
crib	1875	1715
twin bed	4647	4249
full bed	6490	5934
queen bed	7394	6761
king bed	9687	8858

finished sizes

cradle blanket
• W: 15½" × L: 30"
• W: 39.5 cm × L: 76 cm

stroller blanket
• W: 30" × L: 36"
• W: 77 cm × L: 91.5 cm

lap blanket
• W: 36½" × L: 48"
• W: 92.5 cm × L: 122 cm

crib blanket
• W: 42" × L: 52"
• W: 107.5 cm × L: 132 cm

swaddler
• W: 48½" × L: 48½"
• W: 123 cm × L: 123 cm

small throw
• W: 48½" × L: 60"
• W: 123 cm × L: 152.5 cm

large throw
• W: 60½" × L: 72"
• W: 153.5 cm × L: 183 cm

twin bed
• W: 60½" × L: 90"
• W: 153.5 cm × L: 228.5 cm

full bed
• W: 84½" × L: 90"
• W: 214.5 cm × L: 228.5 cm

queen bed
• W: 90" × L: 96"
• W: 229 cm × L: 244 cm

king bed
• W: 118" × L: 96"
• W: 300.5 cm × L: 244 cm

PATTERN SPECS

yarn
- Assorted DK- or worsted-weight wool or wool-cotton yarn
- Lap Blanket size shown in a combination of Brooklyn Tweed DK- and worsted-weight yarns: Shelter, Arbor, Dapple, and Re•Ply Rambouillet

gauge
17 stitches & 28 rows = 4" [10 cm] in blocked stockinette stitch

needles
One 32" [80 cm] or longer circular needle in size needed to obtain gauge
- Suggested size: US 7/4.5 mm

notions and tools
- Stitch marker
- Blunt tapestry needle
- T-pins and blocking wires (optional)

sizing note
Finished dimensions do not include fringe.

fringe note
Finished fringe length is 8" [20.5 cm]. Longer fringe will require more yarn.

special techniques
- Blocking: page 182

stitch patterns

garter pattern
Worked over any number of stitches; 2-row repeat
row 1 (RS): Knit.
row 2 (WS): Slip 1 knitwise WYIB, knit to end.
Repeat Rows 1 and 2 for pattern.

stockinette pattern
Worked over any number of stitches + 6; 2-row repeat
row 1 (RS): Knit.
row 2 (WS): Slip 1 knitwise WYIB, knit 5, sm, purl to end.
Repeat Rows 1 and 2 for pattern.

reverse stockinette pattern
Worked over any number of stitches + 6; 2-row repeat
row 1 (RS): Purl.
row 2 (WS): Slip 1 knitwise WYIB, knit 5, sm, knit to end.

pattern notes
- You will join yarn at the beginning of every RS row (even if you are working with the same color as on the previous row), leaving an 11" [28 cm] tail, and break yarn at the end of every WS row leaving another 11" [28 cm] tail. Tie the RS and WS row tails together, being careful not to tie them too tightly. If you wish to adjust the fringe length, add 3" [7.5 cm] to your desired finished fringe length. The sample finished fringe length is 8" [20.5 cm].
- At the beginning of each RS row, after working several stitches, check the tail length again to make sure it is the desired length.
- After working the 6 Garter Pattern (see Stitch Patterns) rows at the beginning of the blanket, you will work first in Stockinette Pattern (see Stitch Patterns) with the color of your choice. Work Stockinette Pattern for as many rows as you choose in the same color. When you wish to change to the next color, change to Reverse Stockinette Pattern (see Stitch Patterns) and continue for as many rows as you choose in the same color. Continue in the same manner, switching between Stockinette Pattern and Reverse Stockinette Pattern stitch every time you switch colors, and leaving a tail at the beginning of every RS row and end of every WS row.

PATTERN INSTRUCTIONS

Leaving an 11" [28 cm] tail, cast on 66 (129, 206, 155) (206, 257, 180) (257, 359, 384, 503) stitches using your preferred method. For this pattern, we recommend the Long-Tail Cast-On. Break yarn, leaving an 11" [28 cm] tail.

bottom border
note: Color changes are not specified in the pattern; change colors as desired.

Carefully join the new yarn to the cast-on row, leaving an 11" [28 cm] tail, and tie the tail to the cast-on tail. Work in Garter Pattern for 6 rows, joining new yarn at the beginning of every RS row and breaking the yarn at the end of every WS row, leaving an 11" [28 cm] tail for each yarn. Tie pairs of tails together.

main fabric
*When ready to change colors, work in Stockinette Pattern for the desired number of rows with the new color, leaving tails as established.

When ready to change colors, work in Reverse Stockinette Pattern for the desired number of rows with the new color, leaving tails as established.

Repeat from * until piece measures 29 (35, 47½, 47) (59, 71, 51) (89, 89, 95, 95)" [76 (91.5, 123, 122) (152.5, 183, 132) (228.5, 228.5, 244, 244) cm], ending with a WS row.

top border
Work in Garter Pattern for 7 rows, leaving tails as established.

With WS facing, bind off all stitches, leaving an 11" [28 cm] tail.

finishing
Weave in ends invisibly on the WS. For a polished finish, steam- or wet-block (see Special Techniques on page 182) the blanket to the finished dimensions for your chosen size to set the fabric. Smooth out and trim the fringe to your desired finished length.

overlay

designed by Vincent Williams Jr.

This Bauhaus-inspired crocheted throw artfully combines colors to create the appearance of a bold accent stripe overlaid on an abstract composition of black rectangles. Inspired by the layers of transparency in a paned greenhouse, this design will feel right at home in playful, modern spaces. The fabric is worked using basic single crochet stitches, allowing the colorful geometry of the intarsia design to take center stage. The blanket pictured uses four colors, though it's easy to envision ways of exploring the design using six, eight, or more.

skill level

●●●○○
Intermediate

finished size

small throw
- W: 53¾" × L: 57"
- W: 136.75 cm × L: 145 cm

special techniques

- Foundation Single Crochet (fsc): page 183
- Grafting: page 183
- Blocking: page 182

yardage table

blanket size	C1		C2		C3		C4	
	yards	meters	yards	meters	yards	meters	yards	meters
small throw	1311	1199	691	632	621	568	485	443

PATTERN SPECS

yarn

- Worsted-weight wool yarn
- Shown in Brooklyn Tweed Shelter (140 yards/50 g) in colors "Snowbound" (C1), "Cadet" (C2), "Cast Iron" (C3), "Deep Dive" (C4)

gauge

13 stitches & 16 rows = 4" [10 cm] in blocked single crochet

hook

Suggested size: US H-8/5 mm or size needed to obtain gauge

notions and tools

- Blunt tapestry needle
- One set of double-pointed needles (DPNs) in same size as crochet hook and two locking stitch markers (for optional applied I-cord border)
- Bobbins (optional)
- T-pins and blocking wires (optional)

147

PATTERN INSTRUCTIONS

notes

- The blanket is worked flat from the bottom up, using the intarsia colorwork technique. Be sure to always drop the resting colors/working yarn to the WS of the fabric when transitioning to the next block of color in any given row.
- The project begins with a foundation single crochet (fsc).
- This design features an optional applied I-cord border.
- When beginning and ending a color, leave 6-8" [15-20 cm] tails for weaving in.

panel A

row 1 (WS): With C3, fsc 34, with C4, fsc 78, with C3, fsc 78, turn. [190 stitches]

row 2 (RS): With C3, ch 1, sc 78, with C4, sc 78, with C3, sc 34, turn. [190 stitches]

row 3 (WS): With C3, ch 1, sc 34, with C4, sc 78, with C3, sc 78, turn.

row 4 (RS): With C3, ch 1, sc 78, with C4, sc 78, with C3, sc 34, turn.

rows 5 and 6: Repeat Rows 3 and 4.

Break both strands of C3.

panel B

row 1 (WS): With C1, ch 1, sc 34, with C2, sc 19, with C4, sc 7, with C2, sc 52, with C1, sc 78, turn.

row 2 (RS): With C1, ch 1, sc 78, with C2, sc 52, with C4, sc 7, with C2, sc 19, with C1, sc 34, turn.

rows 3-12: Repeat Rows 1 and 2.

Break the strand of C1 that spanned 34 stitches.

panel C

row 1 (WS): With C3, ch 1, sc 34, with C2, sc 19, with C4, sc 7, with C2, sc 52, with C1, sc 78, turn.

row 2 (RS): With C1, ch 1, sc 78, with C2, sc 52, with C4, sc 7, with C2, sc 19, with C3, sc 34, turn.

rows 3-10: Repeat Rows 1 and 2.

Break C3.

panel D

row 1 (WS): With C1, ch 1, sc 34, with C2, sc 19, with C4, sc 7, with C2, sc 52, with C1, sc 78, turn.

row 2 (RS): With C1, ch 1, sc 78, with C2, sc 52, with C4, sc 7, with C2, sc 19, with C1, sc 34, turn.

rows 3-14: Repeat Rows 1 and 2.

Break the strands of C2 and C1 that spanned 52 and 78 stitches respectively.

panel E

row 1 (WS): With C1, ch 1, sc 34, with C2, sc 19, with C4, sc 59, with C3, sc 26, with C1, sc 52, turn.

row 2 (RS): With C1, ch 1, sc 52, with C3, sc 26, with C4, sc 59, with C2, sc 19, with C1, sc 34, turn.

rows 3-22: Repeat Rows 1 and 2.

Break the strands of C3 and C1 that spanned 26 and 52 stitches respectively.

panel F

row 1 (WS): With C1, ch 1, sc 34, with C2, sc 19, with C4, sc 7, with C2, sc 52, with C1, sc 78, turn.

row 2 (RS): With C1, ch 1, sc 78, with C2, sc 52, with C4, sc 7, with C2, sc 19, with C1, sc 34, turn.

rows 3-28: Repeat Rows 1 and 2.

Break the strands of C1, C2, and C4 that spanned 34, 19 and 7 stitches respectively.

panel G

row 1 (WS): With C3, ch 1, sc 34, with C4, sc 26, with C2, sc 52, with C1, sc 26, with C3, sc 52, turn.

row 2 (RS): With C3, ch 1, sc 52, with C1, 26, with C2, sc 52, with C4, sc 26, with C3, sc 34, turn.

rows 3-18: Repeat Rows 1 and 2.

Break the strands of C3 and C4 that spanned 34 and 26 stitches respectively.

panel H

row 1 (WS): With C1, ch 1, sc 34, with C2, sc 19, with C4, sc 7, with C2, sc 52, with C1, sc 26, with C3, sc 52, turn.

row 2 (RS): With C3, ch 1, sc 52, with C1, sc 26, with C2, sc 52, with C4, sc 7, with C2, sc 19, with C3, sc 34, turn.

rows 3-10: Repeat Rows 1 and 2.

Break C3.

panel I

row 1 (WS): With C1, ch 1, sc 34, with C2, sc 19, with C4, sc 7, with C2, sc 52, with C1, sc 78, turn.

row 2 (RS): With C1, ch 1, sc 78, with C2, sc 52, with C4, sc 7, with C2, sc 19, with C1, sc 34, turn.

rows 3-8: Repeat Rows 1 and 2.

Break the strand of C1 that spanned 78 stitches.

panel J

row 1 (WS): With C1, ch 1, sc 34, with C2, sc 19, with C4, sc 7, with C2, sc 39, with C4, sc 13, with C3, sc 78, turn.

row 2 (RS): With C3, ch 1, sc 78, with C4, sc 13, with C2, sc 39, with C4, sc 7, with C2, sc 19, with C1, sc 34, turn.

rows 3-6: Repeat Rows 1 and 2.

Break the strands of C4 and C3 that spanned 13 and 78 stitches respectively.

panel K

row 1 (WS): With C1, ch 1, sc 34, with C2, sc 19, with C4, sc 7, with C2, sc 52, with C1, sc 78, turn.

row 2 (RS): With C1, ch 1, sc 78, with C2, sc 52, with C4, sc 7, with C2, sc 19, with C1, sc 34, turn.

rows 3-14: Repeat Rows 1 and 2.

Break all strands.

panel L

row 1 (WS): With C3, ch 1, sc 34, with C4, sc 78, with C3, sc 26, with C1, sc 52, turn.

row 2 (RS): With C1, ch 1, sc 52, with C3, sc 26, with C4, sc 78, with C3, sc 34, turn.

rows 3-40: Repeat Rows 1-2.

Break all strands.

panel M

row 1 (WS): With C1, ch 1, sc 34, with C2, sc 19, with C4, sc 7, with C2, sc 52, with C1, sc 78, turn.

row 2 (RS): With C1, ch 1, sc 78, with C2, sc 52, with C4, sc 7, with C2, sc 19, with C1, sc 34, turn.

rows 3-6: Repeat Rows 1 and 2.

panel N

row 1 (WS): With C1, ch 1, sc 34, with C2, sc 19, with C4, sc 7, with C2, sc 52, with C1, sc 26, with C3, sc 52, turn.

row 2 (RS): With C3, ch 1, sc 52, with C1, sc 26, with C2, sc 52, with C4, sc 7, with C2, sc 19, with C1, sc 34, turn.

rows 3-16: Repeat Rows 1 and 2.

Break C3.

panel O

row 1 (WS): With C1, ch 1, sc 34, with C2, sc 19, with C4, sc 7, with C2, sc 52, with C1, sc 78.

row 2 (RS): With C1, ch 1, sc 78, with C2, sc 52, with C4, sc 7, with C2, sc 19, with C1, sc 34.

rows 3-6: Repeat Rows 1 and 2.

panel P

row 1 (WS): With C1, ch 1, sc 34, with C2, sc 19, with C4, sc 7, with C2, sc 13, with C4, sc 39, with C3, sc 9, with C1, sc 69, turn.

row 2 (RS): With C1, ch 1, sc 69, with C3, sc 9, with C4, sc 39, with C2, sc 13, with C4, sc 7, with C2, sc 19, with C1, sc 34, turn.

rows 3 and 4: Repeat Rows 1 and 2.

Break the strands of C3 and C4 that spanned 9 and 39 stitches respectively.

panel Q

row 1 (WS): With C1, ch 1, sc 34, with C2, sc 19, with C4, sc 7, with C2, sc 52, with C1, sc 78, turn.

row 2 (RS): With C1, ch 1, sc 78, with C2, sc 52, with C4, sc 7, with C2, sc 19, with C1, sc 34, turn.

rows 3-14: Repeat Rows 1 and 2.

Break all strands of C1 and C2.

panel R

row 1 (WS): With C3, ch 1, sc 34, with C4, sc 78, with C3, sc 78, turn.

row 2 (RS): With C3, ch 1, sc 78, with C4, sc 78, with C3, sc 34, turn.

rows 3–6: Repeat Rows 1 and 2.

Break all working yarns.

finishing

optional applied i-cord border

setup step 1: Join color C3 to the bottom right corner of the blanket. Ch 4, pull up a loop in the back bump of the 2nd, 3rd, and 4th ch from the hook, pull up a loop in the first sc of the first row in Panel A. [5 loops/stitches on hook]

setup step 2: Slip the last 4 stitches from the crochet hook onto the DPN and place the 5th st onto a locking st marker. Slip 1 st onto the hook, ch 1, slip next st onto the hook, ch 1, slip remaining 2 stitches onto the hook, ch 1 tog through the last 2 newly added stitches on the hook (3 loops/ stitches on hook), pull up a loop in the next row on the blanket edge st. [4 loops/stitches on hook]

row 1: Slip last 3 stitches WYIB to DPN, ch 1 through st remaining on hook, ch 1 through next st on DPN, ch 1 tog through the last 2 stitches on DPN, pull up a loop in the next blanket edge st/Panel st. [4 stitches on hook]

Repeat Row 1 instructions across the side edge of the blanket to the top right corner, making sure to work the row instructions with the same color yarn that corresponds to the Panel colorblock that you will pull up a loop through.

To work around a corner, repeat Row 1 instructions three times total, making sure to anchor the last loop in the same Panel st/edge st

Repeat Row 1 instructions around the remaining top, left, and bottom sides of the blanket edge, making sure to work around the corners as listed above, until there is only 1 row left to complete.

final row: Slip 3 stitches WYIB to DPN, ch 1 through st remaining on hook, ch 1 through next st on DPN, ch 1 tog through the last 2 stitches on DPN, place the 3 loops on second locking stitch marker.

ladder up column/i-cord finishing column: With the WS facing you, insert hook into the marked st at the beginning of the I-cord. Using only the bars/ladders as your working yarn, continuously sl st around the entire blanket.

Cut yarn, leaving an 8" [20 cm] tail. Place the remaining 4 live stitches (loop from laddering up + 3 stitches on hold) on a DPN and join to the corresponding 4 stitches from the first row using Grafting (see Special Techniques on page 183).

Weave in ends invisibly on the WS of the fabric. For a polished finish, steam- or wet-block (see Special Techniques on page 182) the piece to size.

quarterline

designed by Seth Richardson

This garter stitch blanket imposes a "zipper" colorblock motif over a ground of broad stripes for an effect both bold and subtle. Choose two individual color pairs—here a light and medium gray combine with a tonal duo of magentas—to achieve the overall effect. Beautiful results can be attained with both high-contrast colors and atmospheric, analogous combinations. Choose an inspiring palette that makes you smile as you explore color theory. The garter stitch fabric keeps the knitting straightforward and meditative—very weeknight- or travel-friendly!—allowing the maker to focus on the soothing stacks of alternating stripes.

skill level
●●○○○
Adventurous Beginner

finished sizes
stroller blanket
• W: 31" × L: 37¾"
• W: 78.5 cm × L: 96 cm

lap blanket
• W: 36¾" × L: 50½"
• W: 93.5 cm × L: 128.5 cm

small throw
• W: 43¼" × L: 63"
• W: 110 cm × L: 160 cm

twin bed
• W: 58" × L: 88"
• W: 148 cm × L: 224 cm

special techniques
• Long-Tail Intarsia Cast-On: page 185
• Icelandic Bind-Off: page 183
• Blocking: page 182

yardage table

blanket size	C1		C2		C3		C4	
	yards	meters	yards	meters	yards	meters	yards	meters
stroller	307	281	307	281	307	281	307	281
lap blanket	489	444	489	444	489	444	489	444
small throw	714	653	714	653	714	653	714	653
twin bed	1347	1232	1347	1232	1347	1232	1347	1232

PATTERN SPECS

yarn
• Worsted-weight wool yarn
• Small Throw size shown in Brooklyn Tweed Tones (140 yards/50 g) in colors "Hollyhock Overtone" (C1), "Hollyhock Undertone" (C2), "Baseline Overtone" (C3), and "Baseline Undertone" (C4)

gauge
17 stitches & 38 rows = 4" [10 cm] in blocked garter stitch

needles
One 40" [100 cm] or longer circular needle in size needed to obtain gauge
• Suggested size: US 8/5 mm

notions and tools
• Blunt tapestry needle
• T-pins and blocking wires (optional)

153

pattern notes

- The blanket is worked flat widthwise, one stripe at a time consisting of an overtone and an undertone of the same colorway. Garter stitch is worked throughout the piece, using the intarsia method to switch tones at the quarter line as you work across the row. In the first section, one-quarter of the width is worked in overtones and three quarters will be worked in undertones. Six stripes in two alternating colorways are knit and then the point of intarsia moves to the right quarter for another six stripes. This sequence is repeated throughout the work, creating a kind of geometric zipper effect with overtones on the right side and undertones on the left side.

- Each row is created with two colors that are joined at the quarter line using intarsia. This is a very simple cross of the yarns so that they twist to prevent a gap in the fabric where the colors meet. For intarsia in garter stitch on the RS, cross the old yarn over the new yarn, pick up the new yarn, and continue knitting the row with the new yarn.

On the WS, bring the old yarn to the front (between you and the work) and cross it over the new yarn. Pick up the new yarn and continue knitting the row. The yarns will wrap around each other on the WS and will create a solid fabric.

- Each stripe uses two of the four colors, and you may break the yarn at the end of each stripe to weave in all the ends when you are finished. If you would prefer to avoid weaving in so many ends and don't mind managing all four colors at once, you can carry the unused color up the wrong side so that it's available the next time you need to switch colors. This can be done on the second stitch so that it's less visible from the edge. This can also be done on the second stitch after the intarsia cross to keep those yarns tidy.

- If you would prefer a slipped-stitch edge to a garter-stitch edge, on each WS row slip the first and last stitches with the yarn in front.

PATTERN INSTRUCTIONS

With C1 and using the Long-Tail Intarsia Cast-On (see Special Techniques on page 185), cast on 33 (39, 46, 62) stitches and then with C2, cast on an additional 99 (117, 138, 186) stitches. [132 (156, 184, 248) stitches total]

stripe A1

setup row (WS): With C2, knit 99 (117, 138, 186), cross old yarn over new yarn; with C1, purl 13 (39, 46, 62).

row 1 (RS): With C1, knit 33 (39, 46, 62), cross old yarn over new yarn; with C2, knit 99 (117, 138, 186).

row 2 (WS): With C2, knit 99 (117, 138, 186), cross old yarn over new yarn; with C1, knit 33 (39, 46, 62).

Repeat Rows 1 and 2 three more times.

stripe A2

Break C1 and join C3. Break C2 and join C4.

row 1 (RS): With C3, knit 33 (39, 46, 62), cross old yarn over new yarn; with C4, knit 99 (117, 138, 186).

row 2 (WS): With C4, knit 99 (117, 138, 186), cross old yarn over new yarn; with C3, knit 33 (39, 46, 62).

Repeat Rows 1 and 2 four more times.

Break C3 and join C1. Break C4 and join C2.

*Work Rows 1 and 2 of Stripe A1 five times.

Work Stripe A2.

Repeat from * 1 more time.

**stripe B1

row 1 (RS): With C1, knit 99 (117, 138, 186), cross old yarn over new yarn; with C2, knit 33 (39, 46, 62).

row 2 (WS): With C2, knit 33 (39, 46, 62), cross old yarn over new yarn; with C1, knit 99 (117, 138, 186).

Repeat Rows 1 and 2 four more times.

stripe B2

Break C1 and join C3. Break C2 and join C4.

row 1 (RS): With C3, knit 99 (117, 138, 186), cross old yarn over new yarn; with C4, knit 33 (39, 46, 62).

row 2 (WS): With C4, knit 33 (39, 46, 62), cross old yarn over new yarn; with C3, knit 99 (117, 138, 186).

Repeat Rows 1 and 2 four more times.

Break C3 and join C1. Break C4 and join C2.

Repeat from ** 2 more times.

***Work Rows 1 and 2 of Stripe A1 five times.

Work Stripe A2.

Work Stripe B1.

Work Stripe B2.

Repeat from *** 1 (2, 3, 5) more time(s).

Bind off all stitches using the Icelandic Bind-Off (see Special Techniques on page 183). When there are two stitches of C3 remaining on the L needle, pick up C4 and complete the bind-off using this color.

finishing

Weave in ends invisibly on the WS. For a polished finish, steam- or wet-block (see Special Techniques on page 182) the blanket to the finished dimensions for your chosen size to set the fabric.

vitraux

designed by Scott Rohr

This quilt-inspired design is a modern interpretation of stained glass. Conceived by the designer as an homage to his father, a master quilter, the blanket's construction translates common quilting techniques like piecing and binding into knitterly vernacular, using short rows to achieve the angular geometry of each panel. The blanket is composed of five separate strips, each worked in a unique color combination. When the strips are complete, they are joined together with vertical strips of garter stitch to create the stained-glass-like framing of the colored panels.

skill level

●●●○○
Intermediate

finished size

small throw
- W: 55" × L: 63¾"
- W: 139.5 cm × L: 162 cm

special techniques
- Provisional Crochet Cast-On: page 186
- Short Rows: German Method: page 187
- Blocking: page 182
- Right Raised Increase (RRI): page 187

yardage table

blanket size	C1		C2		C3		C4		C5	
	y	m	y	m	y	m	y	m	y	m
small throw	242	221	207	189	245	224	195	178	227	208

blanket size	C6		C7		C8		C9		C10		C11	
	y	m	y	m	y	m	y	m	y	m	y	m
small throw	213	195	236	216	207	189	224	205	216	198	763	698

PATTERN SPECS

yarn
- Worsted-weight wool yarn
- Shown in Brooklyn Tweed Tones (140 yards/50 g) in colors "Zest Undertone" (C1), "Zest Overtone" (C2), "Granita Overtone" (C3), "Granita Undertone" (C4), "Vacay Undertone" (C5), "Vacay Overtone" (C6), "Stonewash Overtone" (C7), "Stonewash Undertone" (C8), "Nimbus Overtone" (C9), "Nimbus Undertone" (C10), and "Baseline Overtone" (C11).

gauge
18 stitches & 28 rows = 4" [10 cm] in blocked Stockinette stitch

needles

One 24" [60 cm] circular needle or straight needles in size needed to obtain gauge
• Suggested size: US 7/ 4.5 mm

One 24" [60 cm] circular needle or straight needles and one 40" [100 cm] or longer circular needle one size smaller than main needle
• Suggested size: US 6/ 4 mm

notions and tools
• Size US G-6/4 mm crochet hook and smooth waste yarn (for Provisional Crochet Cast-On)
• Waste yarn or stitch holders
• Blunt tapestry needle
• T-pins and blocking wires (optional)

stitch patterns

stockinette with garter selvedge
Worked over any number of stitches + 2; 2-row repeat

row 1 (RS): Knit.

row 2 (WS): Knit 1, purl to last stitch, knit 1.

Repeat Rows 1 and 2 for pattern.

short row wedge 1
note: When working short-row wedges, hide pulled stitches as they are encountered.

short row 1 (RS): Knit 43; turn.

short row 2 (WS): S&P, purl to last stitch, knit 1.

short row 3: Knit to 3 stitches before pulled stitch from previous RS row; turn.

short row 4: S&P, purl to last stitch, knit 1.

short rows 5-28: Repeat Short Rows 3 and 4 twelve more times.

short row wedge 2
note: When working short-row wedges, hide pulled stitches as they are encountered.

row 1 (RS): Knit.

short row 2 (WS): Knit 1, purl 3; turn.

short row 3: S&P, knit to end.

short row 4: Knit 1, purl 4; turn.

short row 5: S&P, knit to end.

short row 6: Knit 1, purl 9; turn.

short row 7: S&P, knit to end.

short row 8: Knit 1, purl to 3 stitches after pulled stitch from previous RS row; turn.

short row 9: S&P, knit to end.

short rows 10-29: Repeat Short Rows 8 and 9 ten more times.

row 30: Knit 1, purl to last stitch, knit 1.

short row wedge 3
note: When working short-row wedges, hide pulled stitches as they are encountered.

row 1 (RS): Knit.

short row 2 (WS): Knit 1, purl 42; turn.

short row 3: S&P, knit to end.

short row 4: Knit 1, purl to 3 stitches before pulled stitch from previous RS row; turn.

short row 5: S&P, knit to end.

short rows 6-29: Repeat Short Rows 4 and 5 twelve more times.

row 30: Knit 1, purl to last stitch, knit 1.

short row wedge 4
note: When working short-row wedges, hide pulled stitches as they are encountered.

row 1 (RS): Knit.

row 2 (WS): Knit 1, purl to last stitch, knit 1.

short row 3: Knit 4; turn.

short row 4: S&P, purl to last stitch, knit 1.

short row 5: Knit to 3 stitches after pulled stitch from previous WS row; turn.

short row 6: S&P, purl to last stitch, knit 1.

short rows 7-30: Repeat Short Rows 5 and 6 twelve more times.

pattern notes
• The blanket is constructed from five knit columns. The color blocks are created with undertones and overtones of five colors, creating a gradient effect across the columns. German short rows (see Special Techniques on page 187) create the angles of the color blocks. Garter bands separate the color blocks, sometimes with the contrast color, sometimes with the column colors. Garter borders are the vertical strips between columns. They are picked up along the right edge of Columns 1–4, then seamed to their neighbors. Garter borders are also picked up along each outside edge, mitered with increases, then seamed at the corners.
• Break yarn at each color change; do not carry colors up outside edge.

158

PATTERN INSTRUCTIONS

column 1

<u>section 1</u>

With waste yarn and larger needle(s), cast on 44 stitches using the Provisional Crochet Cast-On (see Special Techniques on page 186).

Switch to C1; work Stockinette with Garter Selvedge (see Stitch Patterns) for 36 rows.

Work Short Row Wedge 1.

<u>section 2</u>

Switch to smaller needle(s) and C2; knit 10 rows.

Switch to larger needle(s); work Short Row Wedge 2.

Work Stockinette with Garter Selvedge for 6 rows.

Work Short Row Wedge 1.

Switch to smaller needle(s) and C11; knit 10 rows.

<u>section 3</u>

Switch to larger needle(s) and C1; work Short Row Wedge 2.

Work Stockinette with Garter Selvedge for 36 rows.

Work Short Row Wedge 3.

Switch to smaller needle(s); knit 10 rows.

<u>section 4</u>

Switch to larger needle(s) and C2; work Short Row Wedge 4.

Work Stockinette with Garter Selvedge for 16 rows.

Work Short Row Wedge 3.

Switch to smaller needle(s) and C11; knit 10 rows.

<u>section 5</u>

Switch to larger needle(s) and C1; work Short Row Wedge 4.

Work Stockinette with Garter Selvedge for 16 rows.

Work Short Row Wedge 1.

<u>section 6</u>

Switch to smaller needle(s) and C2; knit 10 rows.

Switch to larger needle(s); work Short Row Wedge 2.

Work Stockinette with Garter Selvedge for 36 rows.

Work Short Row Wedge 1.

<u>section 7</u>

Switch to smaller needle(s) and C11; knit 10 rows.

Switch to larger needle(s) and C1; work Short Row Wedge 2.

Work Stockinette with Garter Selvedge for 22 rows.

Break yarn and transfer stitches to waste yarn or stitch holder.

column 2

<u>section 1</u>

With waste yarn and larger needle(s), cast on 44 stitches using the Provisional Crochet Cast-On.

Switch to C3; work Stockinette with Garter Selvedge for 26 rows.

Work Short Row Wedge 3.

Switch to smaller needle(s); knit 10 rows.

<u>section 2</u>

Switch to larger needle(s) and C4; work Short Row Wedge 4.

Work Stockinette with Garter Selvedge for 40 rows.

Work Short Row Wedge 3.

Switch to smaller needle(s) and C11; knit 10 rows.

<u>section 3</u>

Switch to larger needle(s) and C3; work Short Row Wedge 4.

Work Stockinette with Garter Selvedge for 18 rows.

Work Short Row Wedge 1.

Switch to smaller needle(s) and C11; knit 10 rows.

<u>section 4</u>

Switch to larger needle(s) and C4; work Short Row Wedge 2.

Work Stockinette with Garter Selvedge for 28 rows.

Work Short Row Wedge 3.

section 5

Switch to smaller needle(s) and C3; knit 10 rows.

Switch to larger needle(s); work Short Row Wedge 4.

Work Stockinette with Garter Selvedge for 20 rows.

Work Short Row Wedge 3.

Switch to smaller needle(s) and C11; knit 10 rows.

section 6

Switch to larger needle(s) and C4; work Short Row Wedge 4.

Work Stockinette with Garter Selvedge for 14 rows.

Switch to smaller needle(s); knit 10 rows.

section 7

Switch to C3; work Stockinette with Garter Selvedge for 48 rows.

Break yarn and place stitches on waste yarn or stitch holder.

column 3

section 1

With waste yarn and larger needle(s), cast on 44 stitches using the Provisional Crochet Cast-On.

Switch to C5; work Stockinette with Garter Selvedge for 2 rows.

Work Short Row Wedge 1.

Switch to smaller needle(s) and C11; knit 10 rows.

section 2

Switch to larger needle(s) and C6; work Short Row Wedge 2.

Work Stockinette with Garter Selvedge for 28 rows.

Work Short Row Wedge 1.

section 3

Switch to smaller needle(s) and C5; knit 10 rows.

Switch to larger needle(s); work Short Row Wedge 2.

Work Stockinette with Garter Selvedge for 34 rows.

Work Short Row Wedge 3.

Switch to smaller needle(s) and C11; knit 10 rows.

section 4

Switch to larger needle(s) and C6; work Short Row Wedge 4.

Work Stockinette with Garter Selvedge for 12 rows.

Work Short Row Wedge 3.

Switch to smaller needle(s); knit 10 rows.

section 5

Switch to larger needle(s) and C5; work Short Row Wedge 4.

Work Stockinette with Garter Selvedge for 48 rows.

Work Short Row Wedge 1.

Switch to smaller needle(s) and C11; knit 10 rows.

section 6

Switch to larger needle(s) and C6; work Short Row Wedge 2.

Work Stockinette with Garter Selvedge for 42 rows.

Work Short Row Wedge 1.

section 7

Switch to smaller needle(s) and C5; knit 10 rows.

Switch to larger needle(s); work Short Row Wedge 2.

Work Stockinette with Garter Selvedge for 2 rows.

Break yarn and transfer stitches to waste yarn or stitch holder.

column 4

section 1

With waste yarn and larger needle(s), cast on 44 stitches using the Provisional Crochet Cast-On.

Switch to C7; work Stockinette with Garter Selvedge for 40 rows.

Work Short Row Wedge 3.

Switch to smaller needle(s) and C11; knit 10 rows.

section 2

Switch to larger needle(s) and C8; work Short Row Wedge 4.

Work Stockinette with Garter Selvedge for 8 rows.

Work Short Row Wedge 3.

Switch to smaller needle(s) and C11; knit 10 rows.

section 3

Switch to larger needle(s) and C7; work Short Row Wedge 4.

Work Stockinette with Garter Selvedge for 56 rows.

Work Short Row Wedge 1.

Switch to smaller needle(s) and C11; knit 10 rows.

section 4

Switch to larger needle(s) and C8; work Short Row Wedge 2.

Work Stockinette with Garter Selvedge for 52 rows.

Work Short Row Wedge 1.

section 5

Switch to smaller needle(s) and C7; knit 10 rows.

Switch to larger needle(s); work Short Row Wedge 2.

Work Stockinette with Garter Selvedge for 14 rows.

Work Short Row Wedge 3.

section 6

Switch to smaller needle(s) and C11; knit 10 rows.

Switch to larger needle(s) and C8; work Short Row Wedge 4.

Work Stockinette with Garter Selvedge for 36 rows.

Break yarn and transfer stitches to waste yarn or stitch holder.

column 5

section 1

With waste yarn and larger needle(s), cast on 44 stitches using the Provisional Crochet Cast-On.

Switch to C9; work Stockinette with Garter Selvedge for 56 rows.

section 2

Switch to smaller needle(s) and C10; knit 10 rows.

Switch to larger needle(s); work Stockinette with Garter Selvedge for 34 rows.

Work Short Row Wedge 1.

Switch to smaller needle(s) and C11; knit 10 rows.

section 3

Switch to larger needle(s) and C9; work Short Row Wedge 2.

Work Stockinette with Garter Selvedge for 20 rows.

Work Short Row Wedge 1.

Switch to smaller needle(s); knit 10 rows.

section 4

Switch to larger needle(s) and C10; work Short Row Wedge 2.

Work Stockinette with Garter Selvedge for 34 rows.

Work Short Row Wedge 3.

section 5

Switch to smaller needle(s) and C11; knit 10 rows.

Switch to larger needle(s) and C9; work Short Row Wedge 4.

Work Stockinette with Garter Selvedge for 32 rows.

Work Short Row Wedge 3.

section 6

Switch to smaller needle(s) and C10; knit 10 rows.

Switch to larger needle(s); work Short Row Wedge 4.

Work Stockinette with Garter Selvedge for 22 rows.

Work Short Row Wedge 1.

section 7

Switch to smaller needle(s) and C11; knit 10 rows.

Switch to larger needle(s) and C9; work Short Row Wedge 2.

Break yarn and transfer stitches to waste yarn or stitch holder.

assembly

Wet-block (see Special Techniques on page 182) all columns to 9½ × 60" [24 × 152.5 cm].

internal borders

With RS facing, using smaller needle(s) and C11, and beginning at bottom right corner of Column 1, pick up and knit 262 stitches along right edge of Column 1. Knit 9 rows. Bind off all stitches with a relaxed tension, leaving a tail 4 times the length of the column.

Repeat for Columns 2, 3, and 4. Using tails, sew bound-off edge of each column to the slipped stitches along the left side edge of the column to its right (see Assembly Diagram opposite).

finishing

side borders

With RS facing, using larger needle(s) and C11, pick up and knit 262 stitches along one long side edge of blanket.

next row (WS): Knit.

row 1 (RS): Knit.

row 2: Knit 1, RRI (see Special Techniques, page 187), knit to last stitch, RRI. [2 stitches increased]

rows 3-8: Repeat Rows 1 and 2 three times. [270 stitches]

Bind off all stitches with a relaxed tension.

Repeat for opposite side edge.

top border

With RS facing, transfer 44 stitches from each column to needle. [220 stitches]

Join C11.

row 1 (RS): [Knit 44, pick up and knit 4 stitches along side edge of internal border between columns] 4 times, knit to end. [236 stitches]

row 2 (WS): Knit.

row 3: Knit.

row 4: Knit 1, RRI, knit to last stitch, RRI. [2 stitches increased]

rows 5-10: Repeat Rows 3 and 4 three times. [228 stitches]

Bind off all stitches with a relaxed tension.

bottom border

With RS facing, carefully unzip the provisional cast-ons and place 44 stitches from each column on needle. [220 stitches]

Work as for Top Border.

Sew corner seams.

Weave in ends invisibly on the WS. Steam borders or wet-block entire blanket again to finished measurements to set the fabric.

ASSEMBLY DIAGRAM + COLOR DESIGNATION

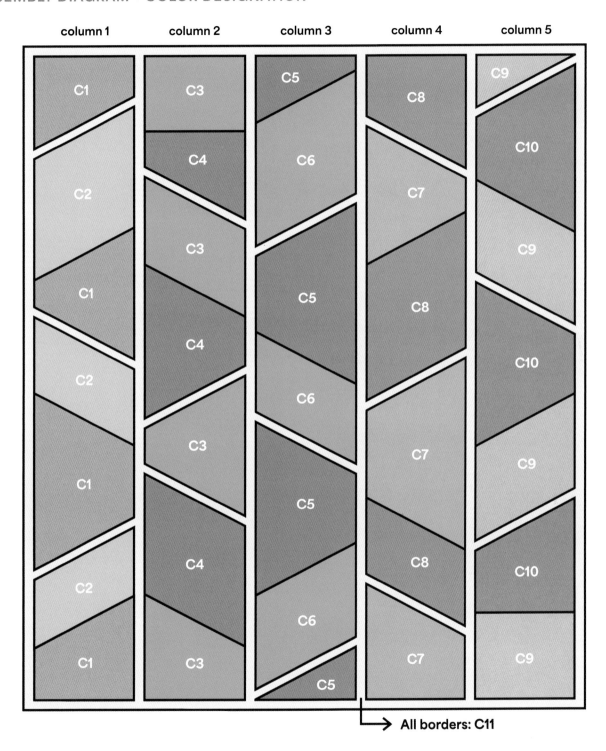

column 1 column 2 column 3 column 4 column 5

All borders: C11

the quilt that started it all

Every meaningful creative project sprouts from the small seed of an idea. For me, it's usually a question I want to answer, or the vision of something that exists in my head that I attempt to craft into reality. The book you hold in your hands began from a simple spark that, over time, was stoked into a creative flame.

In 1997, when I turned fifteen, my mother hand-quilted a beautiful log cabin blanket for me. After high school, the quilt accompanied me through many different phases of early adulthood: college housing in the Pacific Northwest, a decade of New York City apartment shuffles, and now draped over my couch at home in Portland, Oregon. The quilt has been a constant for me through life's ups and downs and has become ever more meaningful over time. As my own skills and mastery of handcrafts have deepened, so too has my appreciation for the skill and artistry that my mother has been cultivating throughout her life.

At the start of the COVID pandemic, I leaned hard on the comforts of home life, and this blanket once again became a source of safety and comfort for me during a very scary time in the world. Knowing I had a blanket that was stitched by my mom helped ease the pain of isolation and separation from friends and family members, including her. During that time, I got the idea of creating a knitted replica of my mom's quilt—a sort of wintry wool counterpoint to the cotton workhorse that has kept me warm for so many years. Soon after, I began translating the original into the Cabin Quilt pattern on the following pages and knitting one of my own.

As I delved deeper into the design process, it became apparent quickly that there were so many different ways this idea could be explored. I then began thinking about how blankets in general are an approachable, accessible canvas for our creative expression as makers. Why not put together a collection of them that would help knitters and crocheters express themselves creatively while nurturing feelings of safety and family in this global time of uncertainty?

This final pattern in the book is the one that started it all and provides a recipe you can use to create a unique and meaningful heirloom in your own life.

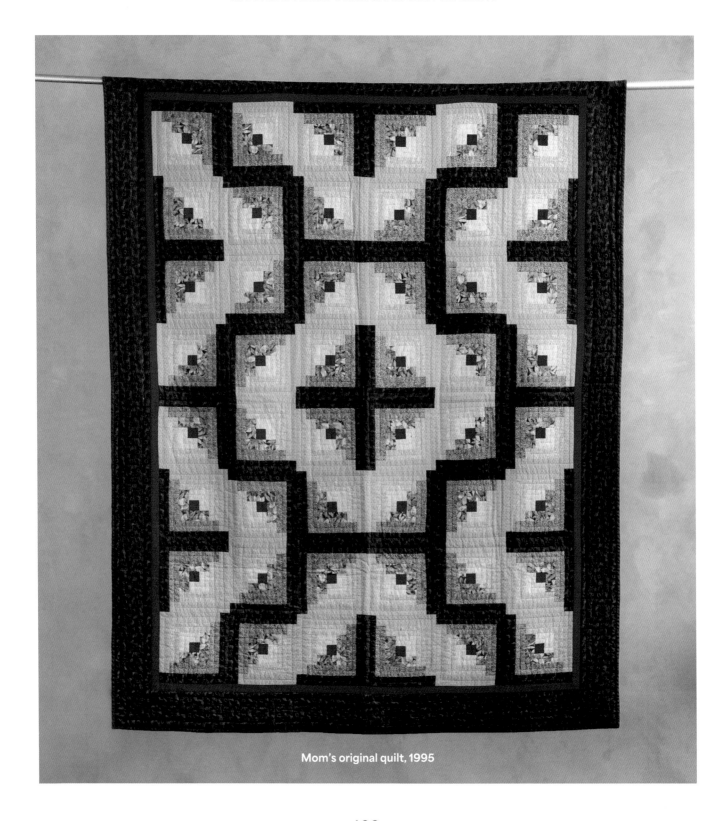

Mom's original quilt, 1995

Jared's knitted tribute, 2023

cabin quilt

designed by Jared Flood

Log cabin quilts rose to prominence as a published quilt style during the American Civil War and have a rich cultural history. Despite a traditional origin and appearance, the log cabin quilt block is one that has lent itself to a mind-boggling number of modern interpretations over many generations of quilters. The traditional block begins with a central square onto which successive strips are added (similar to the construction of log cabin dwellings). The basic blocks can be combined in a dizzying number of orientations with evocative names like "sunshine and shadow," "streak of lightning," "courthouse steps," and "straight furrow," among others.

The modular construction of the log cabin block translates beautifully to knitting, with each small block being its own portable project, while also providing a worthy use for yarn scraps and leftovers. The more colors the merrier!

My pattern has been written for worsted-weight yarns with individual blocks measuring 8½" [21.5 cm] square, though the instructions may be worked in any yarn weight to achieve an alternative individual block size. Make as many or as few blocks as you like to create the finished size blanket you desire. I've photographed two variations—a 16-segment arrangement sized as a baby blanket (or wall hanging), and a larger 48-segment arrangement that can be used as a large throw or bed covering. After completing your blocks, deciding on a finished arrangement, and seaming them together, finish the blanket by knitting on a wide border to frame it all up. Worked in garter stitch, these projects are accessible and, amazingly, use only the classic knit stitch (nary a purl in sight!).

skill level
●●○○○
Adventurous Beginner

finished sizes
swaddler (or wall hanging) (16 blocks)
• W: 43" × L: 43"
• W: 109 cm × L: 109 cm

large throw (48 blocks)
• W: 61" × L: 78"
• W: 155 cm × L: 198 cm

sizing note
Yarn amounts are based on working blocks and multicolor borders in the configurations shown in the sample for each size. Changing the number of blocks, composition of the blocks or borders, or the depths of the borders will change the amount of yarn required for each color.

special techniques
• Blocking: page 182
• Icelandic Bind-Off: page 183

yardage table

blanket size	C1		C2		C3		C4		C5		C6		C7	
	y	m	y	m	y	m	y	m	y	m	y	m	y	m
swaddler (16 blocks)	121	111	96	88	143	131	308	726	286	262	535	489	855	782
large throw (48 blocks)	425	389	344	315	504	461	726	664	746	682	1005	919	2279	2084

PATTERN SPECS

yarn

- Worsted-weight wool yarn
- Swaddler size shown in Brooklyn Tweed Shelter (140 yards/50 g) in colors "Fireball" (C1), "Pollen" (C2), "Delft" (C3), "Klimt" (C4), "Cadet" (C5), "Snowbound" (C6), and "Deep Dive" (C7)
- Large Throw size shown in Brooklyn Tweed Shelter (140 yards/50 g) in colors "Pollen" (C1), "Fossil" (C2), "Bale" (C3), "Snowbound" (C4), "Klimt" (C5), "Pumice" (C6), and "Yellowstone" (C7)

gauge

- 20 stitches & 40 rows (20 garter stitch ridges) = 4" [10 cm] in blocked garter stitch
- One Log Cabin block measures 8½" [21.5 cm] square

needles

One 16-24" [40-60 cm] and one 40" [100 cm] or longer circular needle in size needed to obtain gauge
- Suggested size: US 7/4.5 mm

notions and tools

- Firmly spun sock yarn in a similar color for seaming
- Blunt tapestry needle
- T-pins and blocking wires (optional)

pattern notes

- Worked from the center out, each Log Cabin block is comprised of 13 individual segments. After knitting the small central square (1), each new segment is picked up and worked directly from the previous segment(s). The diagrams on pages 171-173 show the order in which the segments are worked (1–13).
- The pattern calls for 6 garter stitch ridges in every segment. A garter stitch ridge is created after the completion of every pair of rows worked (one RS, one WS); working 6 ridges of garter stitch is the equivalent of working 12 total rows (the pickup row at the beginning of each segment is row 1 of 12).
- After completion of each individual segment of your block, you will turn the work 90 degrees to the right (clockwise) and then begin picking up stitches for the next segment across the top edge of the work. The last segment worked will always be along the right edge of the work when you are beginning a new segment.
- As you build the block, take care to bind off each segment with a relaxed, even tension.
- A single-stitch selvedge is used throughout the project. Whenever you are picking up stitches, pick up into the space between the selvedge (edge) stitch and its neighboring stitch. This creates a clean finished fabric that lays flat and results in a tidy seam on the WS.

PATTERN INSTRUCTIONS
log cabin block

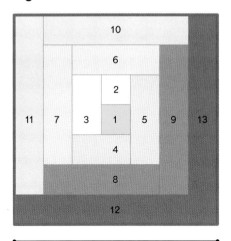

8.5" square

segment 1
With C1 and shorter circular needle, cast on 8 stitches using your preferred method. For this pattern, we recommend the Long-Tail Cast-On.

Work in garter stitch (knit every row) for 6 ridges (12 rows), ending with a WS row.
Break yarn.

segment 2
With C2, continue in garter stitch as established for 6 additional ridges (12 rows), beginning with a RS row and ending with a WS row.

Bind off all stitches until 1 stitch remains on R needle.

segment 3
With RS facing, turn work 90 degrees to the right and continuing with C2, pick up and knit 12 stitches across the edges of Segments 2 and 1, picking up 1 stitch for every garter stitch ridge. At the end of the pickup, cast on 1 more

stitch to R needle using a firm backward loop; you now have 14 stitches on your needle (12 picked-up stitches and 1 selvedge stitch at either side of work).

Work in garter stitch for 6 ridges (12 rows), ending with a WS row. Bind off all stitches in C2. Break yarn.

segment 4
With C3, make a slipknot on R needle. With RS facing, turn work 90 degrees to the right and using working yarn coming from slipknot, pick up and knit 12 stitches across the edges of Segments 3 and 1, picking up 1 stitch for every garter stitch ridge along Segment 3, and 6 stitches across Segment 1. At the end of the pickup, cast on 1 more stitch to R needle using a firm backward loop; you now have 14 stitches on your needle.

Work in garter stitch for 6 ridges (12 rows), ending with a WS row. Bind off all stitches until 1 stitch remains on R needle.

segment 5
With RS facing, turn work 90 degrees to the right and continuing with C3, pick up and knit 18 stitches across the edges of Segments 4, 1, and 2, picking up 1 stitch for every garter stitch ridge. At the end of the pickup, cast on 1 more stitch to R needle using a firm backward loop; you now have 20 stitches on your needle.

Work in garter stitch for 6 ridges (12 rows), ending with a WS row. Bind off all stitches in C3. Break yarn.

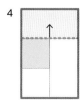

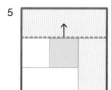

171

segment 6

With C4, make a slipknot on R needle. With RS facing, turn work 90 degrees to the right and using working yarn coming from slipknot, pick up and knit 18 stitches across the edges of Segments 5, 2, and 3, picking up 1 stitch for every garter stitch ridge along Segments 5 and 3, and 6 stitches across Segment 2. At the end of the pickup, cast on 1 more stitch to R needle using a firm backward loop; you now have 20 stitches on your needle.

Work in garter stitch for 6 ridges (12 rows), ending with a WS row. Bind off all stitches until 1 stitch remains on R needle.

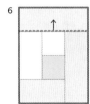

segment 7

With RS facing, turn work 90 degrees to the right and continuing with C4, pick up and knit 24 stitches across the edges of Segments 6, 3, and 4, picking up 1 stitch for every garter stitch ridge along Segments 6 and 4, and 12 stitches across Segment 3. At the end of the pickup, cast on 1 more stitch to R needle using a firm backward loop; you now have 26 stitches on your needle.

Work in garter stitch for 6 ridges (12 rows), ending with a WS row. Bind off all stitches in C4. Break yarn.

segment 8

With C5, make a slipknot on R needle. With RS facing, turn work 90 degrees to the right and using working yarn coming from slipknot, pick up and knit 24 stitches across the edges of Segments 7, 4, and 5, picking up 1 stitch for every garter stitch ridge along Segments 7 and 5, and 12 stitches across Segment 4. At the end of the pickup, cast on 1 more stitch to R needle using a firm backward loop; you now have 26 stitches on your needle.

Work in garter stitch for 6 ridges (12 rows), ending with a WS row. Bind off all stitches until 1 stitch remains on R needle.

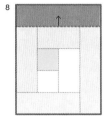

segment 9

With RS facing, turn work 90 degrees to the right and continuing with C5, pick up and knit 30 stitches across the edges of Segments 8, 5, and 6, picking up 1 stitch for every garter stitch ridge along Segments 8 and 6, and 18 stitches across Segment 5. At the end of the pickup, cast on 1 more stitch to R needle using a firm backward loop; you now have 32 stitches on your needle.

Work in garter stitch for 6 ridges (12 rows), ending with a WS row. Bind off all stitches in C5. Break yarn.

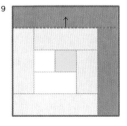

segment 10

With C6, make a slipknot on R needle. With RS facing, turn work 90 degrees to the right and using working yarn coming from slipknot, pick up and knit 30 stitches across the edges of Segments 9, 6, and 7, picking up 1 stitch for every garter stitch ridge along Segments 9 and 7, and 18 stitches across Segment 6. At the end of the pickup, cast on 1 more stitch to R needle using a firm backward loop; you now have 32 stitches on your needle.

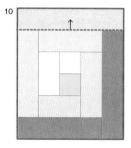

Work in garter stitch for 6 ridges (12 rows), ending with a WS row. Bind off all stitches until 1 stitch remains on R needle.

segment 11

With RS facing, turn work 90 degrees to the right and continuing with C6, pick up and knit 36 stitches across the edges of Segments 10, 7, and 8, picking up 1 stitch for every garter stitch ridge along Segments 10 and 8, and 24 stitches across Segment 7. At the end of the pickup, cast on 1 more stitch to R needle using a firm backward loop; you now have 38 stitches on your needle.

Work in garter stitch for 6 ridges (12 rows), ending with a WS row. Bind off all stitches in C6. Break yarn and proceed with C7.

segment 12

With C7, make a slipknot on R needle. With RS facing, turn work 90 degrees to the right and using working yarn coming from slipknot, pick up and knit 36 stitches across the edges of Segments 11, 8, and 9, picking up 1 stitch for every garter stitch ridge along Segments 11 and 9, and 24 stitches across Segment 6. At the end of the pickup, cast on 1 more stitch to R needle using a firm backward loop; you now have 38 stitches on your needle.

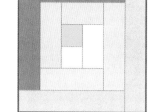

Work in garter stitch for 6 ridges (12 rows), ending with a WS row. Bind off all stitches until 1 stitch remains on R needle.

segment 13

With RS facing, turn work 90 degrees to the right and continuing with C7, pick up and knit 42 stitches across the edges of Segments 12, 9, and 10, picking up 1 stitch for every garter stitch ridge across Segments 12 and 10, and 30 stitches across Segment 9. At the end of the pickup, cast on 1 more stitch to R needle using a firm backward loop; you now have 44 stitches on your needle.

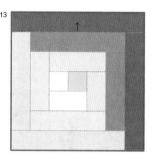

Work in garter stitch for 6 ridges (12 rows), ending with a WS row. Bind off all stitches in C7. Break yarn.

blanket

Repeat instructions for Log Cabin Block until you have made 16 (48) blocks.

finishing

Weave in ends invisibly on the WS. For a polished finish, steam- or wet-block (see Special Techniques on page 182) the blocks to the finished dimensions to set the fabric. You can finish/block your blocks as you go, or wait and do them all at once at the end. Blocking each knitted block will make seaming your blocks easier and tidier.

assembly

confirm your final layout

Before you begin seaming, lay your blocks out and confirm exactly how you would like them to fit together. You may use an arrangement provided here in the pattern, or find your own variation. The blocks can be used in any orientation and position, as long as the overall shape of the blanket is a square or rectangle.

The examples here show the finished layouts of the knitted samples in our photographs. The layout on the left uses 16 knitted blocks while the layout on the right uses 48.

See page 179 for more examples of layout variations.

individual blocks, shown in two colorway variations

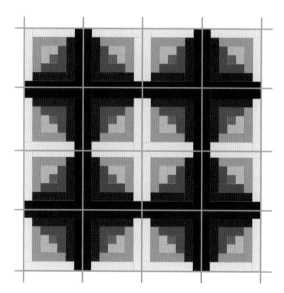

prepare horizontal strips

Divide your blanket's layout into horizontal strips; each horizontal strip is created by seaming together the side edges of the individual blocks in that strip.

In this example, the blanket has a finished width of 4 blocks. Attaching 4 blocks as shown creates one of the four total horizontal strips needed to build this finished motif.

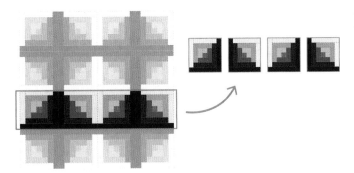

seam horizontal strips

seaming notes:

- Use a tightly spun, strong yarn in a weight slightly lighter than your working yarn for seaming. The seaming yarn may be partially visible from the WS of the work in the finished fabric, so choose a color that coordinates well with your overall color story.
- Use mattress stitch to create all seams in your blanket. When working mattress stitch, use a single-stitch selvedge (rather than a half-stitch selvedge), matching garter ridges and stitches from each side of your seam to keep everything even and straight.
- Work mattress stitch from the RS so that the selvedge stitch seams are on the WS in the finished fabric.
- It is easier to seam blocked blocks (see Finishing).

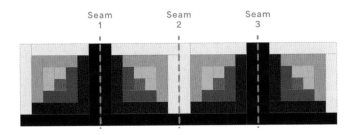

Using mattress stitch, sew together each individual block using short vertical seams across the strip as shown. For a strip that is 4 blocks wide, you will make 3 total seams. For a blanket that is 6 blocks wide, you will need 5 seams, and so on.

combine strips

After you have completed all of the horizontal strips, you will begin stacking the strips from bottom to top, building the finished blanket design in your desired arrangement. The top of one horizontal strip will be joined to the bottom of the neighboring strip using a longer horizontal seam.

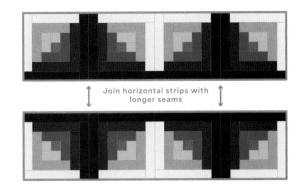

Using mattress stitch, sew together each strip across the width of the blanket as shown. For a design that is 4 strips tall, you will make 3 total seams. For a design that is 8 strips tall, you will need 7 seams, and so on.

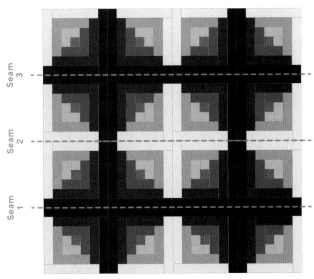

borders

border notes:

- Borders are picked up using working yarn in the same manner you've done all your stitch pickups when working individual blocks: Pick up stitches in a 1-to-1 ratio throughout, whether picking up from a bound-off edge (pick up 1 stitch for every bound-off stitch from the center blanket) or a side edge (pick up 1 stitch for every garter ridge in the fabric).
- You will always work the border along only one of the four sides of your blanket at a time. You will never be working all four sides of the border at the same time. In this way, the border mimics the log cabin pattern of the individual blocks, with each new piece of knitting building directly off the previous section.

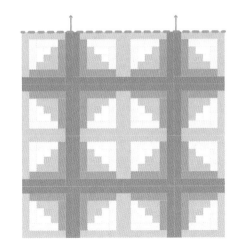

first border

With C6 for Swaddler or C1 for Large Throw (or your preferred border color) and longer circular needle, pick up stitches along one side of blanket as follows: Make a slipknot on R needle. With RS facing, using working yarn coming from slipknot, pick up and knit stitches across edge, picking up 1 stitch for every garter stitch ridge or bound-off stitch (see Border Notes). At the end of the pickup, cast on 1 more stitch to R needle using a firm backward loop.

Work in garter stitch for 5 ridges or to your preferred border thickness, ending with a WS row. Bind off all stitches with a relaxed tension using your preferred method. For this pattern, we recommend the Icelandic Bind-Off (see Special Techniques on page 183).

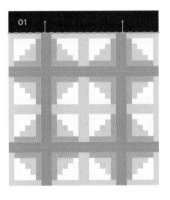 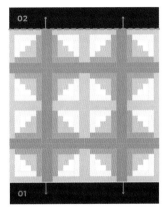

second border

Turn the work 180 degrees and repeat the First Border on the opposite side for Second Border. Work the same number of garter ridges as you did for the first border, ending with a WS row. Bind off all stitches using same method as First Border.

third border

Turn the work 90 degrees and repeat the First Border, picking up stitches directly from the sides of the First and Second Borders as well as the body of the blanket, as shown.

Work the same number of garter ridges as you did for the first two borders, ending with a WS row. Bind off all stitches using same method as First Border.

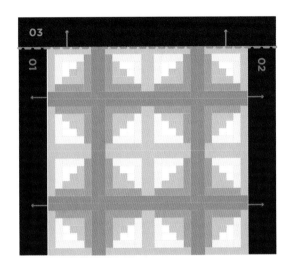

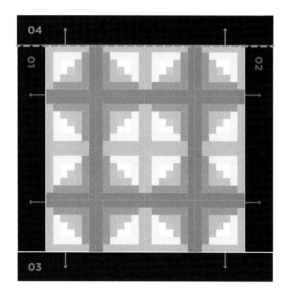

fourth border

Turn work 180 degrees and repeat the Third Border on the remaining side. Work the same number of garter ridges as you did for the First Border, ending with a WS row. Bind off all stitches using same method as First Border.

multicolor borders

Repeat the steps above for every section of border that you would like to work in a different color. You will repeat the process of working each of the 4 border sides one at a time in one color/thickness, then start again using the next color.

Experiment with different colors and border proportions to balance the overall composition of your design. For border inspiration, surf the internet for images of modern or historic quilts to see how their border proportions and colors have been explored.

For our Swaddler sample, we worked the following additional border layers after the first in C6:
• 3 ridges in C4
• 2 ridges in C1
• 13 ridges in C7

For our Large Throw sample, we worked one additional border layer of 20 ridges in C7 after the first in C1.

TRADITIONAL BLOCK ARRANGEMENTS

straight setting

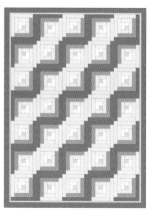

fields & furrows

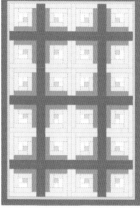

sunshine & shadows

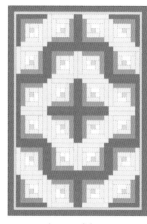

barn raising

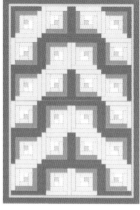

chevron

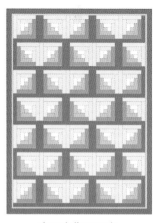

tiered diamonds

179

special techniques

This section includes tutorials for all the special techniques called for in the blanket patterns. Use it as a handy reference for building your skills as you experiment with the projects in the book.

note about charts vs. written instructions: If you prefer working from written line-by-line instructions rather than charts, those can be found online in the Digital Appendix, for all the projects in this book that include charts: https://brooklyntweed.com/pages/knit-and-crochet-blankets-appendix

blocking
wet-blocking

Fill a sink or basin with cold water and a small amount of delicate dish soap or rinse-free wool wash. Submerge the fabric in the water, gently squeezing out any air bubbles. Soak the fabric for 15 minutes, allowing it to become completely saturated.

Drain the sink and remove the fabric. If you have used dish soap (rather than rinse-free wool wash), fill the sink again once or twice to rinse the soap from the fabric. Never place knitting directly under running water.

Squeeze out excess water, taking care not to twist or wring the work. Roll the fabric up between two clean bath towels and firmly press on the towel roll to remove more moisture. Unroll the fabric from the towels—the work should now feel damp but not saturated.

If using blocking wires: Weave blocking wires along each edge of the fabric at regular intervals. Along side edges, you will weave the blocking wires in the running threads between your selvedge stitch and its inside neighboring stitch; weave through every other row for a clean, even edge. Along bind-off edges, weave the blocking wires through the right leg of every stitch in the penultimate row (the last row of knitting before the bind-off). Along cast-on edges, thread the blocking wires through the right leg of every stitch in the first row of knitting (the row you worked directly into your cast-on).

Pin the blocking wires in place on a blocking board or other appropriate surface to the finished dimensions.

If using T-pins: Use as many pins as required on a blocking board or other appropriate surface to hold the fabric to the finished dimensions.

Allow the fabric to air dry completely before removing the wires or pins.

steam-blocking

Lay the fabric flat on a blocking board or other appropriate surface, smoothing it flat with your hands. Using T-pins, pin it to the finished dimensions. Set your iron to the wool setting (medium temperature with steam) and prepare a press cloth (a flat cotton or linen tea towel or piece of cloth of similar weight) by soaking it in water and wringing it out. Lay the damp cloth over the fabric and hold the iron about ½" [12 mm] above the cloth, sending bursts of steam through the cloth. The damp cloth will add extra steam and prevent you from accidentally scorching the fabric. Re-wet the press cloth as needed. Move the cloth and steam each section of the piece. Allow to dry completely before unpinning.

circular cast-on
Make a loop of yarn about 1" [2.5 cm] in diameter (leaving approximately 12" [30.5 cm] for the tail), with the ball end crossing over the tail end, using your fingers

to secure it by pinching where the yarns cross. The ball end should be toward the right, and the tail end to the left. With your needle in your right hand, using the ball end, insert your needle tip into the loop from front to back, wrap the yarn around your needle tip counter-clockwise, and bring it back through the loop. Wrap the yarn around the needle tip counterclockwise again (as though working a yarn over), pass the first loop over the second loop, and then drop it off the needle using your fingers or a second needle. Repeat these two steps until you have cast on the required number of stitches. Distribute your cast-on stitches evenly onto multiple double pointed needles, or onto a long circular needle for Magic Loop, and begin working in the round.

After working several rounds, return to the cast-on and pull the tail to close the loop snugly. Take care not to pull too hard; do not break the yarn when tightening the cast-on.

foundation single crochet (fsc)
Make a slipknot and place on the hook, ch 2. Insert the hook into the second chain from the hook and pull up a loop. Wrap the yarn around the hook and pull through the first loop on the hook to make a chain stitch. Wrap the yarn around the hook and pull through both loops on the hook to make a single crochet. *Insert the hook into the chain stitch and pull up a loop. Wrap the yarn around the hook and pull through the first loop on the hook to make another chain stitch. Wrap the yarn around the hook and pull through both loops on the hook. Repeat from * until the foundation row reaches the desired number of stitches.

grafting
To begin grafting, the pieces to be joined are both live on needles, overlapped with wrong sides facing each other and both open needle tips pointing to the right. Take the yarn coming off the fabric on the back needle and cut it to a length approximately four times the length of the finished seam (use the yarn the piece was knitted with, or attach a new length of yarn). Thread the yarn onto a blunt tapestry needle and follow the steps below, working from right to left (note that you will work into each stitch two times):

step 1: Insert the tapestry needle into the first stitch on the front needle as if to purl; pull the yarn through, but do not slip this stitch from the needle.

step 2: Insert the tapestry needle into the first stitch on the back needle as if to knit; pull the yarn through, but do not slip this stitch from the needle.

step 3: Insert the tapestry needle into the first stitch on the front needle as if to knit, slipping this stitch off the needle. Insert the tapestry needle into the next stitch on the front needle as if to purl and pull the yarn through this stitch, tugging it gently.

step 4: Insert the tapestry needle into the first stitch on the back needle as if to purl, slipping this stitch off the needle. Insert the tapestry needle into the next stitch on the back needle as if to knit and pull the yarn through this stitch, tugging it gently.

Repeat steps 3 and 4 until a single stitch remains on each needle, adjusting the tension of the sewing yarn every few stitches so that it mimics the tension of the knitting. To finish, insert the tapestry needle into the final stitch on the front needle as if to knit, slipping it off the needle. Then insert the tapestry needle into the final stitch on the back needle as if to purl, slipping it off the needle. Pull the yarn through and fasten off gently so as not to distort the stitches.

icelandic bind-off
For a visual demonstration, visit our video tutorial: https://brooklyntweed.com/pages/how-to-knit-icelandic-bind-off-video-tutorial.

step 1: Knit 1 stitch and pass that stitch back to L needle.

step 2: With yarn held in back, insert R needle purlwise through the first stitch on L needle and then knitwise into the front loop of the second stitch on L needle, pulling the second stitch through the first stitch but leaving both stitches on L needle.

step 3: Wrap yarn around R needle tip to knit the second stitch, then drop both the second stitch and the passed-over first stitch from the L needle at once.

step 4: Transfer new stitch back to L needle. Repeat steps 2–4 until 1 stitch remains on L needle. Break yarn and fasten off last stitch.

intarsia method

Intarsia is used to work different sections of color across a row (as for color blocking). A separate length of yarn is used for each section. Wind a length of each color of yarn onto bobbins to prepare for working; refill the bobbins as needed. When changing colors, bring up the new color yarn from underneath the old color yarn, thus twisting them to avoid a hole where the colors were changed.

When working in stockinette stitch: On RS rows, knit to the color change point, and with both yarns at the back (WS) of work, bring the new color up from underneath the old color, and continue knitting in the new color. On WS rows, purl to the color change point, and with both yarns at the front (WS) of work, bring the new color up from underneath the old color, and continue purling in the new color.

When working in garter stitch: Place a removable marker on the RS of work to remind yourself which side is the RS. On RS rows, knit to the color change point, and with both yarns at the back (WS) of work, bring the new color up from underneath the old color, and continue knitting in the new color. On WS rows, knit to the color change point, bring the working yarn to the front (WS) of work, bring the new color up from underneath the old color, bring it to the back (RS) of work, and

continue knitting in the new color (old color yarn left at WS of work).

When you are weaving in the ends during finishing, make sure to sew them in such a way as to avoid a gap where the yarns were cut and a new color joined in.

italian tubular bind-off

For a visual demonstration, visit our video tutorial: https://brooklyntweed.com/pages/how-to-knit-italian-tubular-bind-off-video-tutorial.

step 1: Break your working yarn, leaving a tail about 3 times as long as the width of the piece being bound off. Thread this tail onto your tapestry needle. Insert the tapestry needle into the first (knit) stitch as if to purl.

step 2: From the back, insert the tapestry needle into the front leg of the second (purl) stitch on the needle as if to knit.

step 3: Insert the tapestry needle into the first stitch as if to knit, slipping it off the needle.

step 4: From the front, insert the tapestry needle into the second stitch on the needle as if to purl.

step 5: Insert the tapestry needle into the first stitch as if to purl, slipping it off the needle.

step 6: From the back, insert the tapestry needle into the front leg of the second (purl) stitch on the needle as if to knit.

Repeat steps 3–6 until 1 stitch remains, ending with step 3, adjusting the tension of the sewing yarn every few stitches so that it mimics the tension of the knitting. To finish, insert the tapestry needle into the last stitch as if to purl, slipping it off the needle. Pull the yarn through and fasten off gently so as not to distort the stitches.

italian tubular cast-on

For a visual demonstration, visit our video tutorial: https://brooklyntweed.com/pages/how-to-knit-italian-tubular-cast-on-video-tutorial.

step 1: Make a slipknot (optional), leaving a tail two to three times longer than the desired width of your cast-on. Slip the slipknot or loop onto the needle and hold it in your right hand ready to knit. With your index finger and thumb of your left hand extended to create an "L," position the working yarn in your left hand, with the working yarn draped over your index finger and the tail yarn draped over your thumb, holding the ends against your palm. The yarn is held in a diamond shape, with the slipknot positioned halfway between your thumb and index finger, and the needle tip positioned above the yarns, pointing to the middle of the diamond shape.

Create a Knit Stitch [facing; this will be a purl stitch when turned to the other side]:

step 2a: Wrap the tail yarn over the needle by moving the needle tip outside of the diamond toward your thumb and over the tail yarn, then back to the center of the diamond under the tail yarn.

step 2b: Move the needle tip outside of the diamond toward your index finger and over the working yarn, back to the center of the diamond under the working yarn, then forward under the tail yarn and returning to the center. Keep the loop on the needle and maintain an even tension, ready to cast on a new stitch.

Create a Purl Stitch [facing; this will be a knit stitch when turned to the other side]:

step 3a: Wrap the working yarn over the needle by moving the needle tip outside of the diamond toward your index finger and under the working yarn, then back to the center of the diamond.

step 3b: Move the needle tip outside of the diamond toward your thumb and over the tail yarn, back to the center of the diamond under the tail yarn, then back under the working yarn and returning to the center. Keep the loop on the needle and maintain an even tension, ready to cast on a new stitch.

Repeat steps 2 and 3 until the desired number of stitches have been cast on minus 1 stitch.

To secure the cast-on row and create your final stitch:

If you end with step 2, move the needle tip toward the index finger and insert the needle from left to right under the strand of working yarn behind the index finger, releasing the yarn from the index finger and tightening the yarn to make a backward loop on the needle.

If you end with step 3, move the needle tip toward the thumb and insert the needle from left to right under the strand of the tail yarn in front of the thumb, releasing the yarn from the thumb and tightening the yarn to make a backward loop on the needle.

knitted cast-on

Make a slipknot on L needle to begin. Insert R needle into slipknot and knit a new stitch. Place new stitch on L needle. *Insert R needle into the new stitch on the L needle, wrap strand of yarn around right needle as you would for a knit stitch and pull through, and place this new loop onto L needle; repeat from * until required number of stitches have been cast on. After last stitch has been cast on, slip last stitch purlwise to R needle, bring working yarn to front between needles, return last stitch to L needle, and pull working yarn snugly. Repositioning the working yarn in this way creates a cleaner edge at the end of your cast-on row.

long-tail intarsia cast-on

With your first color, cast on the desired number of stitches using the traditional Long-Tail Cast-On method. When you reach the place where you need to add another color, create a backward loop with the new color, leaving a tail that is long enough to complete the cast-on. Insert the back of the R needle into the loop and bring the loop up all the way over the stitches you just cast on until it becomes the next stitch and the tails of the first color are going through it. This loop will serve as the first stitch of the next color. Tighten the loop and proceed with Long-Tail Cast-On for as many stitches as you need with the new color.

mattress stitch for crochet

Place two blocks side by side with RS facing up. Locate the back loops of the stitches of the last round of each block in the bottom corners. Thread a blunt tapestry needle with seaming yarn cut to 1½ to 2 times the length of the edge. Starting with the chain that makes up the corner ch-1 space, insert the needle tip into the back loop from front to back on one block and then the corresponding loop on the second block, pulling the length of yarn through, leaving a tail long enough to weave in after seaming is complete. Work several corresponding stitches in this manner, leaving a little slack on each stitch. Make sure that your crochet motifs are mirroring each other on each side of the seam. After every few stitches, pull the yarn through firmly to join the blocks, being mindful not to over-tighten the seam, so that the blocks will lay flat. When you encounter seaming a flat length and a previously seamed joint, you may have to skip a stitch or two to compensate for the extra width of the previous seam. When you reach the end of the seam, weave in your end to secure the yarn. Check the tension of your seam, adjusting as needed. Weave in the beginning length of seaming yarn.

provisional crochet cast-on

For a visual demonstration, visit our video tutorial: https://brooklyntweed.com/pages/how-to-knit-provisional-crochet-cast-on-one.

With waste yarn and crochet hook, make a slipknot and place it on the crochet hook. Crochet 5 or 6 chains before picking up your knitting needle.

Holding the crochet hook in your right hand and the knitting needle in your left hand, bring the yarn behind the knitting needle, and with crochet hook held in front of knitting needle, catch the yarn with the crochet hook and draw the loop through the loop that you previously placed on the hook. There is now 1 loop on your crochet hook and 1 stitch on your knitting needle. *Bring the yarn to the back, behind the knitting needle, keeping the crochet hook in front of the knitting needle. Catch a loop of yarn with the hook and draw it through the loop on the hook (1 new stitch has been cast on to the knitting needle and one new chain made with the hook); repeat from * until the desired number of stitches have been cast on to your needle. Note that as you work, the number of stitches will increase on your knitting needle, but you will never have more than 1 chain on your crochet hook.

You now have the desired number of stitches on your needle and 1 chain on the crochet hook. Chain 5 more stitches with the hook (do not catch the knitting needle when making these), then break the yarn, leaving a 6" [15 cm] tail, and draw tail through the last chain. Switch to the working yarn and begin piece as instructed in pattern.

When you are ready to return to these stitches and work in the other direction, undo the chain where it was fastened off and carefully pull out the waste yarn, "unzipping" the stitches. Transfer them to your knitting needle as they are unfastened.

reading charts

For more information on reading charts, visit our tutorial: https://brooklyntweed.com/pages/reading-charts.

Read RS (usually odd-numbered) chart rows from right to left; read WS (usually even-numbered) chart rows from left to right. When working circularly, read all chart rounds from right to left.

Chart symbols represent the knitting as viewed from the RS of the fabric. Review the Legend of each chart to see how a symbol should be worked from the RS when working a RS row and from the WS when working a WS row.

right raised increase (rri)

For a visual demonstration, visit our video tutorial: https://brooklyntweed.com/pages/invisible-right-raised-increase-in-garter-stitch-one.

With R needle tip, lift the purl bump at the base of the first stitch on L needle, place it onto L needle with R leg of the stitch in front, and knit it through the front loop, then knit the next stitch on L needle.

short rows: german method

For a visual demonstration, visit our video tutorial: https://brooklyntweed.com/pages/how-to-knit-german-short-rows-one.

Turn the work at the end of the current short row. Work a slip & pull (S&P) as detailed below on the first stitch of the row following a turn.

slip & pull (S&P):

After a RS row (WS facing; yarn at front of work): Slip 1 stitch purlwise from L to R needle, pull the yarn over R needle to back (as if making a yarn over) and around to front again, pulling tightly so that the two legs of the stitch in the row below are pulled up and exposed on the R needle; keeping tension on the yarn in order to keep the stitch in this position, continue as directed in pattern.

After a WS row (RS facing; yarn at back of work): Bring yarn to front, slip 1 stitch purlwise from L to R needle, pull the yarn over R needle to back (as if making a yarn over) so that the two legs of the stitch in the row below are pulled up and exposed on the R needle, pulling tightly; keeping tension on the yarn in order to keep the stitch in this position, continue as directed in pattern.

To hide the pulled stitches in subsequent rows: Work to the pulled stitch, which will appear as though two loops are linked at their centers, insert R needle into the center of the linked loops, and knit or purl the stitch as usual.

short rows: wrap & turn method

on a RS row:

Slip the next stitch to R needle, pass the yarn from back to front, slip the stitch back to L needle.

Turn to work WS row, passing the yarn to the front of the work. When you work the next stitch, take care to pull the yarn snugly.

on a WS row:

Slip the next stitch to R needle, pass the yarn from front to back, slip the stitch back to L needle.

Turn to work RS row, passing the yarn to the back of the work.

When you come to a wrapped stitch in subsequent rows:

On a RS row: Insert the R needle under the front of the wrap and then knitwise into the wrapped stitch; knit the wrap together with the wrapped stitch.

On a WS row: Insert the R needle from behind, under the back of the wrap, and lift the wrap onto the L needle; purl the wrap together with the wrapped stitch.

slip-stitch selvedge {sss}:

RS rows: With yarn held in back, slip the first stitch of the row purlwise; work as instructed by the pattern until 1 stitch remains, knit the last stitch.

WS rows: With yarn held in front, slip the first stitch of the row purlwise; work as instructed by the pattern until 1 stitch remains, purl the last stitch.

two-stitch slipped selvedge {s2ss}:

On all rows: With yarn held in front, slip the first 2 stitches of the row as if to purl; work as instructed by the pattern until 2 stitches remain, knit the last 2 stitches.

abbreviations

BOR Beginning of round

ch Chain: Make a slipknot and place on hook. Wrap yarn around hook and pull through the loop. Repeat as many times as indicated. Note that the loop on your hook does not ever count as a chain; only the completed chains are counted.

CN Cable needle

dc Double Crochet: Wrap yarn around hook and insert hook where indicated. Wrap yarn around hook and pull up a loop. Wrap yarn around hook and pull through first 2 loops on hook. Wrap yarn around hook and pull through 2 remaining loops on hook.

DPN Double-pointed needle

fsc Foundation Single Crochet (see Special Techniques on page 183)

k2tog Knit 2 Together: Knit 2 stitches on L needle together. [1 stitch decreased; leans right]

KFB Knit Front & Back: Knit into front and then into back of same stitch. [1 stitch increased]

knit 1-tbl Knit 1 stitch through the back loop

knit2y Knit with 2 strands of yarn held together. Knit stitch holding 1 strand each of MC and C1 or C2 together.

L Left

pm Place marker

R Right

RDD Raised Double Decrease: Slip 2 stitches from L to R needle at the same time as if to k2tog, knit 1 from L needle, pass the slipped stitches over stitch just worked. (2 stitches decreased; centered)

RRI Right Raised Increase (see Special Techniques on page 187)

RS Right Side: The public side of the fabric, i.e., the side of the fabric that will be visible when the garment is worn. In projects with reversible fabrics, RS will be assigned specifically at the beginning of the pattern.

{SSS} Slip-Stitch Selvedge (see Special Techniques on page 187)

{S2SS} Two-Stitch Slipped Selvedge (see Special Techniques on page 188)

S&P Slip & Pull: Used in German Short Rows (see Special Techniques on page 187)

sc Single Crochet: Insert hook where indicated, wrap yarn around hook and pull up a loop. Wrap yarn around hook and pull through both loops on hook.

sl st Slip Stitch Crochet: Insert hook where indicated. Wrap yarn around hook and pull through both the place the hook is inserted and the loop on the hook.

sm Slip Marker

sp Space

SSK Slip, Slip, Knit 2 Together: Slip 1 stitch knitwise from L to R needle, replace stitch on L needle in new orientation then knit 2 stitches together through the back loops. [1 stitch decreased; leans left]

WS Wrong side

WYIB With Yarn in Back

WYIF With Yarn in Front

YO Yarn Over: When to be followed by a knit stitch or knit decrease, bring yarn to front, then over top of R needle from front to back, leaving yarn at back and creating one new stitch. When to be followed by a purl stitch or purl decrease, bring yarn to front, then over top of R needle, returning yarn to front and creating one new stitch.

note: See chart legends in each pattern for abbreviations not listed here.